Parkinsons

- the slippery slope to dementia

by

Bill King

For my wife

© Bill King 2021

(This version printed 14 February 2022)

REVIEWS

I found your book interesting, engaging, entertaining, and at times very moving. What made it particularly poignant is the fact that I do of course know both you and your wife personally, and although you hid her identity I could clearly recognise the person that I knew so well.

I am sure the written account only gives a flavour of everything you have had to go through, and all the pain that you suffered at seeing a loved one deteriorate in this way. Being able to put all this down on paper will, I'm sure, be of considerable benefit to others who might find themselves in this situation. (Murdo Fraser, MSP)

Most of us think we understand Parkinsons but in reality we don't have a clue, unless you live with a family member and have to deal with everything it throws at you, every single day, as you watch your loved one change in front of your eyes.

This is not an easy read in places and I found it emotionally challenging. I felt I was being re-educated, to my shame, as I was one of those who wasn't aware of or didn't understand the obstacles and difficulties 'Bill King' has had to contend with as he lovingly cared for his wife.

None of us knows what lies in store for us, and perhaps that is for the best in some ways, but this book brings to the fore love and despair in equal amounts. I would have no hesitation in recommending you buy it and let others know about it. (Provost Dennis Melloy, Perth and Kinross)

I read the book in two sittings which maybe gives you an indication of how interesting I found it. It certainly opened my eyes more to the challenges carers face trying to deal with a loved one coping with this awful illness and it just makes me more determined to try and do more. (Raymond Jamieson, Carers Hub Manager, PKAVS)

I have just finished reading your book. Thank you for allowing me to share your experience. Having worked in a care home followed by a spell in home care, I have witnessed this scenario many times, also personally, with each of the main carers being brought into a hopeless situation.

This has been a sensitive, touching read and an experience echoed by millions throughout the land, but you have given a little light relief and understanding to the harsh reality and the book gives a true insight to make others feel they are not alone. (LMG)

You have given your wife love by the bucket load. It is clear that it has been a love match. Will she remember this? Who knows, but you will know this and I sincerely hope it will eventually bring you some comfort.

In the greatest way you have bared your soul as well as giving information of great value. I cannot tell you how impressed I am with the content. For me it strikes the perfect note. It is informative, touching and with the degree of humour necessary. I thought you expressed yourself very well. I am sure it will resonate with many readers. (MH)

The sequel to this book, *Dementia – what every carer needs to know*, is now available to read from Amazon, either as a Kindle or a paperback.

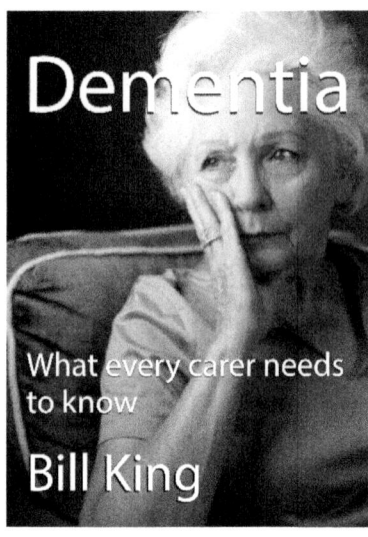

Table of Contents

Author's note 8

Introduction 11

Chapter one – Our story 18

Chapter two – Before the storm 37

Chapter three – Being the main carer 52

Chapter four – Help! 58

Chapter five – The trivial round, the common task 67

Chapter six – Respite 74

Chapter seven – The psychotic episode 77

Chapter eight – Keeping your head above water 79

Chapter nine – Confronting the issues 92

Chapter ten – Guilty or not guilty? 97

Conclusion 105

The challenges of the full-time carer
(A selection of helpful and not-so-helpful quotes)

We make a living by what we get, we make a life by what we give.
(Winston Churchill)

Never believe that a few caring people can't change the world. For, indeed, that's all who ever have.
(Margaret Mead, anthropologist)

There are only four kinds of people in the world. Those who have been caregivers. Those who are currently caregivers. Those who will be caregivers, and those who will need a caregiver.
(Rosalyn Carter)

Non nobis solum nati sumus.
(We are not just born for ourselves – Cicero)

We've put more effort into helping folks reach old age than into helping them enjoy it.
(Frank Howard Clark, screenwriter)

Old age is not so bad when you consider the alternative.
(Maurice Chevalier)

Too bad that all the people who know how to run the country are busy driving taxicabs and cutting hair.
(George Burns)

To care for those who once cared for us is one of the highest honours.
(Tia Walker)

As you get older, three things happen. The first is your memory goes, and I can't remember the other two.
(Norman Wisdom, comedian)

It is not the load that breaks you down. It's the way you carry it.
(Lena Horne)

To the world you may be one person. But to one person you may be the world.
(unknown)

You must learn from the mistakes of others. You can't possibly live long enough to make them all yourself.
(Sam Levenson)

We are all in the gutter, but some of us are looking at the stars.
(Oscar Wilde)

You can't have everything. Where would you put it?
(Steve Wright)

No one has ever become poor by giving.
(Anne Frank)

(There are more semi-helpful quotes at the end of this book.)

Author's note

This book charts the progress – if that's the right word – of Parkinsons as it heads towards dementia in the case of my wife, now in her seventies and in a nursing home. Along the way, I have picked up a fair amount of bitter experience in coping for many years as her main carer.

Anyone who thinks that it is easy watching the woman you have loved devotedly for several decades declining and slipping away from you is cordially invited to try the experience for themselves.

At times, it can be overwhelming, at others almost too painful to bear, and in these pages I have sought to set down what I have learned and experienced in the hope that it will be of some help and support to others facing an inevitable and increasingly challenging situation. I can offer no easy solutions, as there are none.

All I can try and do is to ease a little the pain of other men and women going through similar experiences. If I have achieved that, it will have made this book worthwhile.

I refer to financial amounts and legal situations which held good in Scotland in 2021. Elsewhere in the UK, the terms and conditions can vary quite a lot, and they may change over time.

I have released this effort into the wild as an inexpensive eBook and paperback, so as to give it maximum accessibility. Royalties go to local dementia and related charities.

If you are inclined to make an additional donation, do send a gift to your favourite charity in this field, preferably for a sum slightly greater than the book costs.

As ever many thanks to my beta readers Margaret and Liz for their sharp eyes and continuing support.

I am using a pseudonym for the author's name and that of my wife to help retain our privacy. There is a YouTube presentation based on the book available at this address: https://youtu.be/NUkW5Aou1y0.

The book will have occasional improvements and additional material added. The website will contain advance copies of this material (www.locheesoft.com/parkinsons).

One further comment before we get going: On reading the manuscript through, I find that I tend sometimes to give the impression that I am commanding you to do things. Apologies if that is so, as I am simply seeking to encourage you to take certain steps and think in positive ways.

I am also doing my best not to commit the heinous offence in mental health circles of telling you to 'pull yourself together'. Those are about the least desirable words to utter to anyone in a particularly difficult life situation. I know that from personal experience, and if I do give such an impression, I apologise in advance. I would normally go on the naughty step for that, but I understand that it is fully booked for my many other transgressions.

Introduction

This is a personal account of my faltering attempts at being a carer for my wife over the decade and more since she was diagnosed with Parkinsons and, more recently, with dementia. I don't claim to be a professionally qualified expert on the subject, I just hope that my experiences will shine a light into other folks' dark places as they go through similar experiences to mine. What I do claim is expertise in being a carer and in knowing the person I care for.

Parkinsons is such a shape-shifting enemy, which strikes different people in a wide range of ways and at varying rates of deterioration. But somewhere in the mix there lurks a commonality of experience which I hope to share with you in these pages and which might strike a chord in your own isolated journey as a carer, if you are in that role.

Perhaps the most insidious aspect of the disease is that it sort of creeps up unawares, especially in its earlier phases, and the carer imperceptibly adjusts to a daily but invisible alteration in the symptoms and the way in which they affect both carer and person cared for.

Those adjustments keep on being made and increase the burden on the carer little by little as the months and years go by. If you baulked at my use of the term 'isolated' a little while ago, as you yourself may be surrounded by a circle of support in the shape of professionals, family and friends, the challenges which you face personally and privately cannot be fully shared with others. They remain yours and yours alone. I hope my advice may lighten that load just a little, or at least make it more tolerable.

An additional problem for me was that when the whole business began to get serious I was in my seventies, with a wife ten years younger. The way I try to explain the consequences of being of advanced years is that we as human beings tend to have a fixed amount of energy and time in the day to perform all the tasks that have to be completed, partly for the person with Parkinsons, partly for yourself. In addition, that 'you time' is vital, a space to unwind in, to think of something else and, as they say, do your own thing. There's a lot more about that in Chapter five.

The trouble is that, as the more elderly carer continues down his or her own slippery slope into old age, the amount of time in the day for which you have the energy and ability to function shrinks rapidly as the burden and demands of being a carer increase, until one fine day you reach a tipping point when you literally run out of time and energy and emotional capital. At that moment a quantum shift in your life and that of the person you're caring for occurs, which sadly adds greatly to the intensity of this crisis and the severity of your pain and sense of guilt, and that can so easily cause you to drift into depression or worse.

Before I go any further, there's a language problem or two to sort out. It's quite tricky to come up with the right word to describe 'the person being cared for', without creating too much of a mouthful, and I nearly decided to employ a word I invented for family use, namely, 'caree'.

Then I was going to settle for 'sufferer', but if you are not familiar with the technical use of the word, it does have overtones which imply that the person going into the doctor's surgery is defined by their illness, rather than being a human being who happens to have Parkinsons.

In the end, I settled for the rather long-winded 'person you're caring for', which covers siblings, grandparents, husbands and wives and any other combination of circumstances, and I have altered this revised version of the book accordingly.

I note in passing that one glossy report on carers states that you must not use the term sufferer as that is demeaning. Apart from the fact that such an edict smacks of the current tyranny of non-allowable words and phrases, I actually road-tested this on my wife who stated that sufferer was a pretty good descriptive term.

When 'the person you're caring for' enters a care home the terminology becomes less fraught: you'll find I tend simply to use 'resident' in such cases.

Another little word I have some problems with is 'journey', which has been tainted by over-use in those grisly TV talent shows promising fifteen minutes of fame for aspiring magicians, dancers, comedians, and songbirds. As an aside, the word derives from the French 'journey', the distance which you can travel in a day, although it's now come to refer to a trip far longer than that.

However, I can't find a satisfactory alternative, so you

and I will have to put up with it. I draw your attention to another term I use: 'absentee carer'. This refers to the carer's position when the person you're caring for enters a care home.

You will also note that I call Parkinsons a 'disease'. I rather like to call a spade a spade rather than a convenience for digging, and although I do recognise that it has so many different faces that it could well be called a syndrome, I'm sticking with disease. By the way, I omit the apostrophe as so many folk nowadays refer to the disease simply as Parkinsons, and it looks cleaner on the page.

Another term I dislike is 'issues', referring to problems confronting people with mental health difficulties, which for me trivialises the situation, but it's so widely used I'll have to go along with it, despite my reservations.

And finally on the vocabulary front, I really do draw the line at the term 'partner', particularly now that same sex marriage has been legalised. It's OK if you are not married, but why do many married folk feel coerced by political correctness to use 'partner' despite that? Perhaps I have just answered my own question.

Can I stress that I put fingers to keyboard originally in an attempt to help me come to terms with and make sense of the experiences I have been through, and I make no special claims for my views and offers of practical advice. It doesn't really matter if you accept or reject parts of what I have to say, I simply ask that you give some thought to my suggestions in the earnest hope that they will be of help and support to you.

What I cannot do is to ease your burden or take it away. You can assemble an army of professionals and others about you, but the core of the situation remains unaltered: the person you have come to know and cherish is gradually slipping away from you, and that is the unkindest cut of all.

This book, then, is quite unlike the vast majority of self-help bibles which operate along these lines: they tell you that you have an intractable problem, they have an all-embracing solution and if you follow their words of wisdom, you will at the end emerge blinking into the sunlight utterly revived and ready for action, and with your head held up high. At this point, you are usually invited to transfer large sums of money to the advertiser's off-shore account.

No can do. Parkinsons is a one-way trip, and in later years it can slip into psychosis, dementia and worse, and there no magic bullet to fire at it. Anyone who claims that there is a neat get-out-of-jail-free card for this disease is simply lying. All I aspire to do is to try and make your journey more tolerable by sharing with you my experiences, warts and all, and offering you what comfort I can.

Here's one general point I'd like to raise before we go any further. Because of the closely interlocking relationships between so much of what follows, can I apologise in advance for a little repetition creeping in here and there. In my days as a lecturer, I used to tell my students that I never let incoherence or repetitiousness get in the way of my lecturing. So please be generous to me in that respect.

Life, as I am nowadays accustomed to say, is a four-letter word, describing a strange and unpredictable tale with a sad ending, which over the years becomes sadder still. We as a human race really have only ourselves to blame.

Fifty years and more ago folk worked until they were 60 or 65 if they were lucky to get that far, then they retired and within a couple of years their gold watch was being fought over by their heirs and creditors. Now we hang on for far longer, well past our sell-by dates, and as a consequence we suffer from a raft of degenerative diseases in which the competition for the nastiest is pretty tough.

It is unfortunately clear from the actions of government downwards that we as a society have not yet found a satisfactory way of humanely coping with an ever-growing population of older folk and providing them with the care and dignity they deserve without bankrupting them or ourselves in the process.

Parkinsons is up there with the worst of the degenerative diseases, not least because it's a silent killer which wreaks its havoc gradually over time. I know, the medics claim you don't die *of* Parkinsons, you die *with* Parkinsons, but it is a co-conspirator in a downwards path which can have only one conclusion.

In the text that follows, I have changed names (including my own) and been unspecific about places, employment, and so forth, in order to maintain our privacy. I begin with a background story, suitably anonymised, to give you the broad outline of our own journey through life, and how a contented retirement was transformed into something quite different.

The one thing we do all have in common is that unexpected intrusion of Parkinsons into the later years of our lives. The outcomes and the distress it brings are broadly similar. I then offer a number of chapters dealing with specific aspects of the disease and how to manage them and hopefully stay sane at the same time. I do hope that my scribblings provide some support and consolation for you.

Chapter one – Our story

It started with a twitch. An invisible twitch. For many months, neither of us thought much about it, but it bugged my wife a good deal, so we kept on nagging the medics until one fine day a doctor in our Health Centre referred her to the Neurology department in the local University hospital. Maybe, I guess, in the hope that they could make it go away. However, things didn't quite work out like that. Then it was that the twitch became something far more sinister, and the whole direction of our lives together was irrevocably altered. A tipping point, if ever there was one.

By the way, if you detect that the first sentence in this chapter strikes a vaguely familiar note, you are right. It's an oblique nod in the direction of that popular singing combo of yore Hot Chocolate and their number containing the words: 'It started with a kiss...Never thought it would come to this.' The first part of the quote is a fond memory of the past, and the second could be taken as a bitter-sweet reflection on the trials and tribulations of late stage Parkinsons.

Our relationship had started out so well, too, and it came about in a completely unexpected manner for both of us. I was on my merry way to Norway to address a conference, and the delegates met up at one of those bland hotels lining the outer edge of Heathrow airport, triple glazed against the raucous din of constant take offs and landings. It was an annual event, and I'd been working as a freelance consultant for this company for some time, giving a talk at each of their shindigs. Everything seemed normal.

I met some old friends and colleagues and quite a few new ones. Most of the attendees would be keen to listen and learn, but I knew that a small band of trainee alcoholics amongst them were determined not to draw sober breath until they were back on the plane home. All went according to plan until, that is, my turn came to sign in officially for the trip with the new PA to the manager of the company's English branch, whom I had only met thus far on the phone.

OK, so most of us turn our pretty noses up at the very notion of love at first sight, and buy into all the grown-up stuff about getting to know someone gradually and developing a wholesome deeper relationship over time, etc, etc. Taking it steadily and all that, one button at a time, as I might say flippantly. Don't believe a word of it.

I toddled up to Rusalka, as I discovered the new PA was called, and gave her my name, rank and number for the flight the following morning. She signed me in and then for some reason she touched me on the arm, held on to it gently for a moment and looked up at me. I looked back at her, and from that moment I was a lost cause. Hopeless case. Hook, line and sinker.

At the time I was in an OK marriage which was getting much less OK by the week, but that wasn't the reason. I didn't even recognise that I was becoming semi-detached and that a better kind of tipping point for me was just round the corner, to mix a metaphor. I rationalised it as falling for her gorgeous face with an amazing smile and a hint of Eastern Europe about her features.

Only later did I actually get to know that she was in fact second generation Ukrainian, a daughter of immigrants who came over in 1946 to start a new life away from the horrors of war and forced labour on a farm in Germany. Hence the unusual name. But it wasn't her face that did it. Nor was it that I 'fancied' her physically. So unlike me, but it never even occurred to me in that moment.

It was (don't laugh) as if I had somehow recognised in that brief fragment of time that she was the woman I wanted to spend the rest of my life with. At first, I didn't even know if she was married or single, childless or a mother of ten, but I had by some mysterious process hoovered up from her simple glance everything I needed to know.

Go on, mock if you will, but hands up all those of you who have ever found yourselves in a similar gobsmacking situation. Hmm, I thought so, quite a lot of you.

I was told once that an uncle of mine, turning up for his first working day in a northern city in his newly promoted position in the insurance business, was walking through the main office when his eye was drawn to one of the typists. He said to himself, 'That's the girl I'm going to marry.' Maybe this propensity does run in the family, but I'm not prepared to arrange a YouGov poll on the topic. Oh, and by the way, he did marry the girl.

Oslo was cold, really cold. Minus ten or fifteen. But it was dry rather than unpleasantly damp unlike snow in the UK tends to be, usually the wrong kind of snow for the trains and everyone else. Over there, instead of fighting the conditions or regarding them with bemused puzzlement, the locals embrace them and just get on with it.

A year or two earlier when the conference delegates all stayed in an old-fashioned hotel in the city centre, my room looked out on a side street and I could observe the taxis returning to join the queue for new fares, hurtling in their snow tyres down the street and performing sudden U-turns into the taxi stand with the grace of swans in the ballet. Do not try that at home.

On this particular occasion, though, we were in one of the poshest hotels in Norway, in the hills above the capital city and not far from the ski jump where the local team had triumphed in the 1952 winter Olympics. The whole atmosphere was laid back and unfussy.

In fact, one evening I happened to be in the main entrance hall when the King turned up for an evening meal and was greeting fellow guests. No big deal. It was so informal, so human in scale and no one made a song and dance about royalty in our presence. Just another pleasant and unexceptional evening in frozen Norway.

After breakfast the next morning, I wandered out with Rusalka on to the packed snow outside the main portico and as a reddish sun struggled to light the clear blue sky a Scandinavian Airlines plane rose in the air, soared round in a half circle, and headed for Heathrow or other points west.

It was a magical spectacle. I turned to her and said, 'I

find you totally fascinating.' Yeuch. I was always the one for the inept chat-up line. But that was the best I could accomplish with my tongue tied.

Fortunately she managed not to have a fit of the giggles, and we arranged to meet up as soon as possible after our return to the UK. And, in case those among you with a prurient curiosity are craving to know, during the brief three-day stay Nothing Happened. Whether or not it was for want of trying, I am going to draw a veil over that and let you guess. Put yourself in my shoes.

Later, it turned out that there were a couple of less than minor obstacles to overcome. I was, as I said, already married. She was, I soon discovered, also married but getting divorced and had two children.

She lived and worked in Northtown (as the more observant among you might guess, this is a made-up name to maintain anonymity), I worked hundreds of miles away, so that was when things got a bit complicated.

We managed to communicate early most mornings by phone. I was usually up and away at first sparrow fart (as folk delicately put it), to get some real work in before the great unwashed turned up and demanded education, and in that time we were able to talk together. Not much, as a friend of hers would tend to listen in, but we did stay in very regular touch, as well as by post (remember that?).

Anyway, I still knew little about her, whether she lived in a squat or a mansion. And she didn't know a great deal about me, either.

The scene now shifts to the first floor dining room of a nearby hotel. It was lunchtime, and liquid refreshment and snacks littered the table between us. My colleague and good friend the Professor of English sat opposite me. He became, for better or worse, my confidant, my agony aunt. I poured out the whole tale to him and he listened quietly.

You could almost hear the cogs whirring away in his head, as this fine medieval scholar finally harrumphed and said, 'Well, Bill, you have a choice. Either Plan A or Plan B.'

I could almost hear them coming, tough words of wisdom from a crusty old man seared by years of cynicism being passed on to a brand new professor still very damp behind the ears. 'Plan A is to keep her as a mistress, Plan B is to go the whole hog, tell Alice what is going on, and opt to marry Rusalka and live happily ever after.' (Or not, I could hear in his voice. Of his own marriage, the less said the better, but alcohol was involved.)

At least I had found someone to talk to in that time of self-doubt and confusion. He and I occasionally used to chatter the time away in the sitting room at his home, me perched on an uncomfortable antique chaise longue, he leaning back in an ancient wing chair.

On one occasion, he passed me a wine glass which looked unusually chunky. It had a crest of some kind on it, with the letter 'N' was engraved underneath.

I asked what it signified and he replied nonchalantly that he had found and purchased a few of them in an antique shop for a song. They were, he added, Napoleon's military campaign glasses.

Hence the solid build quality. That was hardly the sort of thing to tell someone downing their third or fourth glass of expensive Chardonnay. I clutched on to it for dear life thereafter.

A few weeks later Rusalka and I finally met again in a hotel in Northtown one wet and wintry evening. I had persuaded Alice that I was just having another Important Meeting with the manager of the company I freelanced for, and I took the one direct rail service per day and duly turned up.

I can assure you that this was not the kind of situation I was accustomed to, walking a high wire without a safety net and not knowing what was at the end of the journey, if anything. Plan B was well underway.

Faint heart never won fair lady, but in my case it was a seriously clumsy ticker that somehow did the trick. I clicked open my posh Samsonite attaché case and presented her with the largest box of chocolates I could fit into its black leather interior. Not a good move.

She took it, then told me blushingly that she was on a diet, but that didn't stop her from setting it carefully on one side for her return journey. Then I handed her a photograph which I had taken of a red rose. OK, not the grandest gesture, I'll admit, but you'll find that fresh flowers inside a stuffy briefcase for hours on the long train journey down to Northtown is not a good idea either.

My excuse is that those were the days before every main railway station had been turned into a shopping mall. My offerings seemed to work, and despite my clodhopping efforts, things went rather well after that. Fade to black, as they used to do before Netflix insisted on showing us (nearly) every gory detail. Later, I told her I had two adopted children from a previous marriage and that things were not too bright for me in my current relationship.

Sorry to be a bit vague at this point, but I have to avoid treading on some rather sore toes. I was overwhelmed by her genuineness, her confident tone, her distinctive voice, her warmth and – how long have you got? I was well and truly a prisoner of love, to quote Perry Como, a songster from the early days of those American TV shows which were imported over here to fill up the programme schedules.

We went down to the hotel carvery, bright lights and a babble of loud conversation covering our tentative interchanges. She had just signed divorce papers and lived in a terraced council house. Juggling work and child care was a real challenge, and her greatest blessing was that she lived directly opposite a fish and chip shop, and Northtown is a pretty good place to enjoy such delicacies.

No gourmet affectations like deep fried Mars bars, simply the signature dish of cod battered golden and cooked until it curled up like those images of salmon leaping up a waterfall. Her very well-fed children were a girl, eleven, and a boy, nine.

The time after that when we met again, believe it or not, we were organising her move up to the frozen north with the two children, all her possessions and offspring. (Plus a guinea pig, but that doesn't even merit a walk-on part in this tale.)

You may think this was totally crazy on our part, which I suppose it was, but there was an overwhelming sense of inevitability and happy anticipation about the whole business which caught both of us by surprise. Mother-in-law to be, though, was at first not amused. Fast forward several happy years with just the usual teenage screams and tantrums. Not from us two, I hasten to add.

Now, we thought, life would become easier. Then a close family member suddenly fell victim to a severe mental health episode. Someone rang to tell us that he was currently in the psychiatric ward of a local hospital.

That led to many years of problems and heartache, but our love for each other was strong enough to carry us through. Corny, but true.

I recall the father of a young man in similar circumstances telling me gloomily, 'This will affect your marriage.' By which he meant it will totally screw things up if the mother became utterly obsessed with caring for her wayward son and left the fractious hubby on the sidelines, as had happened in his case. Fortunately, that did not happen to us.

So life bumped along, and then for a while mother-in-law came to stay. I won't bore you with the details, but there she was 'one fine day', as the lady in *Madama Butterfly* sings. She was an archetypal matriarch, with a fixed glare that could kill at twenty paces.

Her problem was that she wasn't in control of our house. Rusalka and I would not tolerate it. So there were some bruising encounters, but it sort of worked out.

They chattered happily away in quick-fire Ukrainian most of the time, so I wasn't particularly sure what was going on. I was gradually making sense of bits of the language, as it is fairly close to learning Russian, which I had started to attempt many years before. After a few months, mother-in-law had to move into a care home as her health declined.

We had struggled to cope with a relative's mental issues for so long it seemed like normal, but someone please tell me what normal is really like and can I have some.

Those are just noises off, as they say in the theatre, so let's focus on Rusalka and her cruel date with destiny and her twitch, which came to us all as a complete surprise.

I'd just taken early retirement and we were enjoying 'proper' holidays for the first time. The situation with the ill relative had begun to stabilise and we were able to travel and enjoy retirement, even though I was busily editing a national computing magazine from home, communicating with the editorial office and the printer by fax, that ghastly invention that has since deservedly died but apparently still lives on to this day in the NHS and elsewhere. Get a grip, people, and join the twenty-first century.

Just when it seemed all was going well for a change, along came that fateful afternoon when she drove off in her car to the hospital to discuss her 'twitch' at a neurology appointment. We didn't think there was much cause for concern, and to my later great regret I couldn't accompany her, as I had a key committee meeting which I couldn't squirm out of as I was chairing it and a few heads badly needing knocking together. So the afternoon droned on and I came back home to the former mill owner's house we had purchased from a local doctor.

It was in need of some TLC, but we were instantly won over by the airy high-ceilinged rooms (except in the maid's bedchamber upstairs, of course) and the splendid Norwegian broad pine staircase with a stained glass window on the half landing depicting a local beauty spot.

In those days, no one had yet come up with the smart phone, so I waited to see if she could find a phone booth (one of those red boxes with a pay telephone in it – remember them?) to call me. She did, and the news was not great. In fact, it was pretty terrible.

The twitch that no one could observe because, as she said repeatedly, it was 'inside her arm', was not as innocuous as we thought, it was actually the first symptom of Parkinsons. Ouch. No wonder the poor lass was upset, even though we hadn't at that time got a clue about the full implications of what Parkinsons was and how it was going to affect her over time.

Google was but a babe in arms, and all we had was the Concise Oxford dictionary and other works of reference. I experienced an unpleasant flashback to a telly documentary in the days of flickering black and white 405 lines, or maybe it was BBC2 with a massive 625 lines resolution. It had depicted some poor bloke with Parkinsons, struggling to cope with wild uncontrollable movements which could not at the time be managed because of the lack of the modern medication which had come on stream when Rusalka was diagnosed.

The shock of witnessing some stranger cut down in their prime by this awful disease had for some reason stuck in my mind and suddenly rose up again to haunt me. My dear departed mother used to say, with that know-it-all nod and a wink beloved of the matriarchs of her generation, 'Some things are meant to be, my dear.' Oh, really. Do you think you could you have a word with whoever it is makes this stuff up for us?

I must have still been tucked up in my mother's womb when the Phoney War occurred at the start of World War Two, so I don't remember what was later correctly described as the quiet before the storm. Some quiet, some storm, as Churchill might have said.

We lived more or less happily through our own Phoney War of Parkinsons which lasted for some considerable time, three or four years in fact, and only gradually did the real symptoms begin to manifest themselves. And even then, they didn't seem too bad, just an occasional shaky leg. I recall one of her consultants saying that for someone with Parkinsons she seemed to be one of the lucky few whose illness progresses at snail's pace.

And so it did, until we came to the first of a number of bumps in the road. In the middle of the night, Rusalka woke up yelling with pain and quite inconsolable. It was pretty clear that something other than Parkinsons was behind this sudden bolt from the blue.

The out-of-hours doctor turned up during the wee small hours, produced an evil-looking syringe-full of analgesic and plunged it into her lower back. That seemed to do the trick.

A painful trip to the hospital X-ray department came soon after, and there it was confirmed that she had two crushed lumbar vertebrae which were causing her a spot of bother. It never rains, but it pours. That didn't help to hold back the Parkinsons, and from then on she went about with a curvature of the spine which became progressively more pronounced as the weeks and months went by.

One of the things medics like to do to patients is to give them a drip feed, but unfortunately they also tend to extend that practice to the patient's carer. We get information drip fed to us, a stage at a time, as it were, and we are not told about the whole story of the illness at the beginning, so we don't know what we are in for. It's a case of 'You know we said this stage is as bad as it gets', but don't get told that the next one is worse still until it turns up out unannounced.

Why don't the professionals just come out and tell us what the destination can be of a long-term disease like Parkinsons? Because I suppose no one wants to mention the dreaded D-word until the last possible moment (when it's too late to readily adjust to the idea). Gradually matters went downhill, accelerating down the slippery slope, heading towards that D-word, dementia.

The worst moment on her journey was a severe psychotic episode, another unsignposted stopping point on the journey to God knows where, which caused her to lose complete touch with reality, and it was apparently not uncommon with Parkinsons. The diagnosis was delirium, which sounds like some Victorian affliction to be managed by laudanum, but which is characterised by a clutch of unpleasant symptoms.

You can guess that I was told that after the event too. I really don't want to mention this next bit, but I feel I must in order to demonstrate what a seriously disturbed individual can do and the potential harm that can occur.

Somehow, she had got hold of one of the extensions to the house phone. She called 999 to tell the police that at that moment I was beating the living daylights out of her. You can imagine the largely unpleasant thoughts that skittered through my mind, which was half shredded into mush by the situation anyway, having to cope with this on top of her crisis, summoning the doctor urgently and all the palaver that goes along with it.

Quite soon after, the blue and white patrol car, lights flashing, charged up our driveway, and I thank my lucky stars that the two young policemen on board, bless them, actually listened to me, and when they saw her screaming and yelling they recognised that I was no wife beater. But an accusation like that can be as bad as being condemned as a paedophile. It could be entirely untrue, but mud sticks and there's no smoke without fire, as the wise-asses say.

So she ended up in a locked ward in the local psychiatric hospital, ironically the same institution in which her relative had spent a long, long time. Visiting was a nightmare, as she would tell me with all the venom at her command that I was deceiving her, bedding half the women in the local town and generally acting the playboy.

That apparently is a classic response by a Parkinsons victim in that situation. But have you seen half the women in the local town? I wondered.

Gradually she improved when she came back home, suffered two further less severe episodes on the back of UTIs (Urinary Tract Infections), after I'd been her carer for what seemed like for ever, since Big Ben was a wristwatch, as they say. At this point, I had learned my first really harsh lesson as an unpaid carer 24/7, which you too will almost certainly have to come to terms with.

The closer you are to the person you're caring for, the more opprobrium is heaped upon you, from a variety of sources. And between you and me, the chief carer really can get it in the neck from the person you're caring for. I know, I have been there, got the bloodied T-shirt and the film rights to go with it.

After that, it took some months until, having been seriously leant on by the GP, social workers and members of the CMHT (Community Mental Health Team), I was forcibly pinned down and told that I was breaking up under the stress, that if something wasn't done about it, I might well be the next guest of the local psychiatric hospital after her. A consummation devoutly to be avoided. What choices did I face?

Before answering that I must tell you how I arrived at this particular tipping point. The answer, oddly, is very gradually, and this can easily happen to anyone in a similar position. Let me explain it this way. If you have grandparents who visit their grandson every six months, their first words on greeting him will be, 'Hasn't he grown a lot and changed?'

And you say to yourself, No, not really. And then you recognise it's all been caused by that four-letter word 'time'. Small incremental changes day by day add up to a huge change after six months. And that is what happened in my journey as a carer.

To lighten the tone for a moment, it reminds me of the doting grandparent who allegedly proclaimed, 'You wouldn't recognise little Johnny, he's grown another foot.' (Joke alert.) That is precisely what happened to me, when I realised how far things had developed.

I don't mean I ended up like the design on the Isle of Man flag, but I had travelled from point A to point B without realising how the gradually increasing pressure of a worsening disease plus the passage of time equals a knackered carer who will end up going to hell in a handcart, if he or she isn't brought up short and forced to recognise that they cannot continue like this.

All of which leads me to the hardest decision I've ever had to take in a long lifetime.

They – social workers plus Parkinson's nurse plus CMHT specialist nurses – told me Rusalka had to go into respite care for a fortnight to give me an essential break from caring. Either that, or I would end up as one of their customers too.

No way, I responded. I fought like a cat trying to struggle its way out of a ball of wool it had itself rearranged into a cat's cradle. But my resolve, such as it was, was weakening.

It was a classic case of not seeing the mote in someone else's eye for the Brazilian rainforest in your own. And I knew it. But I had to be told. And so, too, did Rusalka have to be informed of where she was heading.

At this point I was again drip-fed the information: first, I was persuaded to let her have a go at respite care for a fortnight, and only then was I informed that a nursing home was clearly the appropriate place for her to remain for the foreseeable future and that the appropriate place booking had been made. That was a real body blow for me.

To make the situation slightly less chaotic, Rusalka and I had drawn up mutual Power of Attorney agreements the year before, and now I had full POA for her, as she was deemed incompetent by the medics. I hate POAs.

I had held a POA for my mother and had then felt the full force of bureaucracy bearing down upon me until I nearly screamed for mercy. Apart, that is, from the huge responsibility of being in sole charge of someone else's affairs and finances. More of POAs in Chapter two.

But I did finally have to admit that I had run out of road. I was exhausted, tearful and heading for depression. When one of the community mental health team asked me how I felt, I answered, to my own amazement, 'I am broken.'

Those three little words just slipped out to my surprise and embarrassment. No stiff upper lipped Briton cares to admit that degree of hopelessness, but if you ever feel so utterly drained, you are not alone. Admit it. As I put it in retrospect, I wasn't at the end of my tether, I was witnessing my tether disappearing way into the distance and had no means, it seems, of grasping it and getting back up on my feet.

Asking for help when you can manage no more, that's the first step in beginning to cope with a new situation which for the former full-time carer can be even more daunting. I thought ironically back to a poster I once saw pinned to the wall of one of those gloomy, dusty, old-fashioned hardware stores: 'I walked under a dark cloud and a voice in the cloud said to me, "Look up. Things could get worse." So I looked up, and lo, things did get worse.'

How do you tell the love of your life that she is to go into a nursing home, with you heavily involved in the decision-making process? I had sincerely sworn to her repeatedly that she would return to hospital over my dead body (which, I now suspect, could be arranged), but I had not expected that this extraordinarily painful turn of events would ever confront us.

I had envisaged myself bumbling along and continuing to manage things indefinitely as I had for the past decade or so. I recalled that, some while before, she had come up to me and asked quietly, 'Are you going to put me into a home?' My innocent reply was, 'Certainly not. You *are* in a home, love. Now. Yours.' But, as some wise man must have said, the one thing you can't predict is the future.

In many ways, I suspect it's a blessing, as most of us would run screaming in the opposite direction if we had a crystal ball. As Woody Allen once said, I don't mind dying one day, I just don't want to be there when it happens.

Chapter two – Before the storm

There is one crucial point I'd like to make about preparing for what happens before your partner is diagnosed with Parkinsons or some other serious affliction, or as soon thereafter as possible. If you and the person you are caring for have not already done so, you must at the very first sign of a diagnosis, when they are still of sound mind, appoint a solicitor and request mutual POAs (Powers of Attorney) to be drawn up, giving you long-term authority over health care and general matters, including finance, when the awful day dawns on which he or she has to be issued with a certificate of incapacity, provided by the GP.

Looking further ahead, it is equally important for both of you to write and sign wills. The absence of a proper will really can cause all kinds of bother – and expense.

Do not be overawed by the prospect of meeting with a solicitor. Remember, you are the customer and you should approach the occasion with confidence. Solicitors don't bite, and any inclined to do so would soon be kicked out of their professional associations.

Also, don't be afraid to ask the solicitor questions. These professionals are there to deal with such matters on a regular basis, and they must defend your interests. And, remember, you are paying the bill. Note that we are resident in Scotland and the law and practice is different from that in the rest of the UK. Check the appropriate government, NHS and local authority websites for accurate localised information.

You may both baulk at the very notion of a POA, but I can assure you that it is absolutely essential. It may burn a hole in your finances, but that is nothing compared to the problems which can arise if you fail to take this essential precaution. If you are on benefits or a low income, financial support may be available. Ask the solicitor about that, or check with your local Citizens' Advice Bureau office.

There is one additional point you have to get your head round: What if both of you become too frail to manage your affairs? In that eventuality, we designated our eldest son to take over the POA powers for us both.

Do keep the documents from the solicitor somewhere safe, as it could be months or years before you need them, and do also do undertake the following preparations to make life a little easier for yourself when that day dawns. Produce a few photocopies of the POA or, if you have a computer with a multifunctional printer, scan the POA into a subfolder, and there it can rest until it is needed.

Believe me, this makes life a whole lot easier when you are required to show it to others, but it doesn't always instantly cause a Harry Potter magic wand to be waved which can resolve every problem.

It was pretty dire for me back in the 1990s when my mother became ill, as everyone then demanded a certified copy of the POA, and they were not always returned. Now electronic advances have made life slightly less tiresome. One annoying obstacle I encountered arose when I needed access to a deposit account in my wife's name.

OMG, as the younger generation exclaim in their text messaging. I presented our building society, which shall be nameless, with an electronic copy of the POA and filled in a blizzard of forms (or so it seemed).

As an aside, I am completely baffled as to why one agency is content with a colour facsimile, whereas another demands a photocopy, as that is allegedly more reliable. Names of agencies have been redacted to protect the guilty.

It appeared that the building society specialist team dealing with such matters was very busy. Muttering something under my breath about them getting more staff or improving their procedures, I had to let nature take its course, and it dragged on for a whole month until they completed the process. Four weeks are an eternity in a situation where you are in a crisis and trying to cope with all manner of other challenges.

When I finally acquired their reluctant acceptance that I wasn't a scammer or fraud of some kind, I still had to submit myself to extra fiddling around with my debit card and the card reader in order to access the information.

Then I discovered that if I wanted to switch back to the main account, I couldn't. I would have to log out altogether and log back in again. No comment, but I was reminded of the tale of the bricklayer and the barrel of bricks.

For those of you long enough in the tooth, you may remember the name Gerard Hoffnung. He was a well-known, highly gifted comedian and musician in the last century who held celebrated humorous concerts in the Royal Festival Hall, including one featuring a concerto for hosepipe and orchestra.

The memorable occasion I want to refer to, however, is his address to an Oxford Union debate, at which he recounted the sad tale of a bricklayer's letter to his employer recording his attempts to bring a barrel of bricks down from the roof of a building, using a pulley and line.

He goes through a series of traumatic mishaps, as the barrel shoots up and down, with him on the other end of the rope, being at one stage lighter than the barrel, then heavier, until he ends up bloodied and defeated with the words 'At this point I must have lost my presence of mind,' as in despair he lets go of the rope, causing the barrel to come crashing down on his head.

I felt a bit like that when I finally struggled through the process of implementing a POA with the building society. And that was just one of the organisations I had to deal with.

That phrase from the bricklayer's tale about 'losing my presence of mind' crops up quite a lot in my dealings with bureaucracy. The worst trouble I had was trying to make sense of my wife's medication.

She was taking enough pills to sink a battleship, but even worse, the pill pushers were not all the same person, namely, the general practitioner as you might expect. Some were issued by a hospital consultant, others via different agencies, and there were demarcation disputes galore.

Maybe I exaggerate a tad, but it's stressful enough to be in charge of delivering medication regularly and accurately without having to cope with the complexities of where it comes from and when the fax for the order will actually turn up from the consultant, and whether that request bypasses the GP and goes straight to the pharmacy.

This is particularly challenging when the Parkinsons meds she was taking needed to be administered five times a day, out of sync with most regular medications. And then, when we agreed to switch to a weekly tray of pills which was provided for her through the pharmacy, the contents could be two weeks and more out of date in their provision, and, of course, their trays only had four slots per day. I had to administer the five a day meds separately.

On one occasion this confusion resulted in doses of two pretty hefty antipsychotic drugs being inadvertently prescribed in the trays at the same time, which, if I hadn't got sharp eyes, could have caused quite a few nasty problems. How that sneaked past the pharmacist, I'll never know.

Do not get me started on the confusions relating to the position of the poor pharmacist in this merry-go-round of guess the medication. My unspoken reaction is that this was an acute case of too many chiefs and not enough Indians.

Everyone was in charge, but only of one part of the patient's case and at a different level in the hierarchical structure of the NHS. BTW, to borrow another messaging favourite, the last line of the bricklayer's letter to his employer, after enumerating all the bumps and bruises he had suffered ran as follows: 'I respectfully request sick leave.' I know how he felt.

Another very important point is now coming up. Everyone is different here, and I can only speak for myself, so you take from what follows all that you need and forget the rest. Think long and hard of the practicalities of running a house solo when the person you're caring for no longer lives there.

Do you know the whereabouts of the fuse box, and can you operate the dishwasher, washing machine and tumble dryer? For years I hadn't a clue how the washing machine and dryer functioned, but I had it all written down for me, and now I am an old hand at washing my own stuff and dealing with the bedding.

Names and contact numbers for plumbers, electricians and joiners can be a lifesaver, too, especially ones with an emergency out of hours number, also those of doctors, social work offices (especially their out of hours service, if any), and so on. I cannot overstress how important all that can be. As the politicians say, it's always best to mend the roof when the sun is shining.

OK, you'll say, disaster only happens once in a blue moon, but if a blue moon appears with your name on it, you could be in serious trouble. Also, be aware of the emergency number of your water and electricity suppliers in the event of water cut-offs and power breakdowns. It is advisable to invest in a Calor gas heater or similar, and a small camp stove for boiling a kettle.

We suffer from quite a few electricity cuts out here in the country, with strong winds regularly knocking down power supply poles, especially in the winter, and farmers digging electric cables up with their JCBs.

I presume the system varies depending on the supplier, but in our case we were designated as a household with special needs by our electricity company, and that helped in relation to resumption of supply.

Do not be lulled into a sense of false security by the fact that you yourself have never had a flood in the house, either from equipment failure or ice in pipes melting after a cold snap. That's what insurance is all about, folks. It can never happen, you might say, but, remember, neither could Parkinsons. Do be aware of the various points in the house and outside where you can switch the mains water off in the event of a problem.

Let me bore you with three near disasters in our own house. First, we came back from a fortnight in the sun (our favourite place for acquiring sunburn was the Canary Islands), when I heard the sound of rushing water coming from somewhere above in the house.

Like spit from a bugle, as they say in Yorkshire, I shot upstairs and found that the cistern controlling water flow in the toilet there had failed, causing a mini tsunami to gush out – into the toilet bowl, as it happened by pure chance, so no lasting damage was done.

The second near miss came one day when I was doing some DIY in a nearby room. Suddenly, I thought I could hear the roar of the Niagara Falls in full flood. I went to investigate, and in the shower room I discovered that a flexible pipe to a hand extension to the shower had failed and ruptured. By good fortune it was hanging in its place over the pan of the shower, so that none of the water – yet – had started flooding out over the rest of the floor.

However, the pan was rapidly filling up. By the way, I often wonder why they never bother to turn the Niagara Falls off at night. It would save a lot of water and be much more restful.

Disaster number three nearly did cause a very serious accident. Before the shower room boasted a specially extended shower stall with grab handles and the rest, there was a bath to one side and a small shower set in a corner.

Fortunately, we hardly ever took a bath, because when the side panel was removed to perform the upgrading, lo and behold the mega-brain who had originally fitted the bath had omitted to connect the outlet pipe from the bath itself, so if the bath was filled and emptied, the water would simply be deposited on the wooden floor beneath from where it would seep through into the foundations.

The wooden flooring had rotted to the point where the

next innocent person to have a bath would almost certainly have caused it to collapse through the floor, inflicting unknown but probably unpleasant and potentially serious injuries. Unfortunately, we had no written record of the name of the company which had been chosen to perform that simple task a decade and more before.

Don't get me started either on the chapter of accidents which resulted in two fire engines turning up once in the middle of the night to deal with a house full of smoke. On this occasion the cause was faulty electrical equipment. The blue moon had our names on it that night, too. So the moral of the tale is: Don't be smug and say that it cannot happen to me.

Accidents are things that do occur once in a while, so mitigate their impact and in particular the physical and mental damage they can do. Being a carer is tough enough, so don't go out of your way to make it any more challenging.

Let me now turn to the potentially contentious issue of money. Our marriage has been one where we have shared everything, so there has been no problem managing bank accounts and the pounds and pence generally. Money can be quite a flash point, and not just between partners.

In addition, you should be aware of the amounts the person you're caring for is allowed to have in what the powers that be are pleased to call 'savings' in their name and joint names, before the local council gets its greedy paws on it and makes you pay some or even all of the costs of full-time care until you run out of money.

I know, it punishes those who have carefully built up savings for their old age, and protects the feckless who may have drunk, holidayed or gambled their excess cash away. Also it is an extremely blunt instrument.

If you squirrel a few thousand away, it is most often no more than a short-term fund for a rainy day, when white goods, for example, require replacement. That can hardly be explained away by the powers that be as long-term savings.

The system can also unfairly burden folk whose houses, if they own them, have been lived in for many years and you find the value has sneaked up without you realising it.

That will be a real problem particularly if the person you're caring for is the sole owner of the property. If that is the case and you are resident there, do check on the consequences. I believe tricky issues can arise if the carer and person cared for are not married, the carer wishes to continue living there, and the house is solely in their name.

And do also recognise that there is an unpleasant little clause in officialdom's approach to savings, the so-called 'deprivation of assets'. If you are deemed deliberately to have moved money out of a claimant's account in order (in their view) to reduce the amount to a level below one of their set financial thresholds, you are penalised because, in their words, you still have 'notional capital'. So don't try it, but if there is good reason why you have transferred money out of an account, ensure that transactions are noted down and explained, with evidence where necessary.

As soon as the person you're caring for enters into full-time care, there are a number of financial steps you need to take. First, make sure you have with you the relevant paperwork when contacting officialdom. You will also need their National Insurance number.

The DWP (Department of Work and Pensions) should be contacted if a PIP (Personal Independence Payment) has been granted to them, especially at the advanced level, and also if you have a Motability hire vehicle, which you may be able to continue to use, if you are a designated driver, after the person you're caring for goes into care.

In addition, the DWP should be made aware of your circumstances so that adjustments can be made to the winter fuel payments you receive. As a council tax payer, you may be entitled to a discount as a single occupant, and in general you should keep an eagle eye open for any other financial implications of changes to your circumstances.

When the dust has settled, there is another matter which ought to be addressed. I know it sounds a touch ghoulish, but everyone's stay on this planet is limited, so they tell me, and one fine day we will all be pushing up the daisies, to coin a phrase. It is sensible, if you have not already done so, to make plans for funeral arrangements, dealing with the nature and cost of the ceremony, and the plot of ground if there is to be a burial or two, and so forth.

Believe me, it saves a lot of additional hassle at a time when your mind is hardly on practicalities like this, and in any event, the care home might request information about such plans for their records.

One particular beef I have about the financial situation in Scotland, which may be replicated elsewhere in the UK, is that you can have a house full of paid carers helping to manage and deal with various needs, and only pay a little or nothing towards the cost.

However, the moment the prospect of a full-time care home rears its ugly head, you can hear the insistent rattle of the corporation collecting tin. After all the high-level talk of merging nursing and social care, there's a logical flaw lurking somewhere in that little lot.

Currently, in Scotland in 2021, if you have savings or capital over £18,000 you pay a pro rata amount towards residential care, and if that amount exceeds £28,750 you are deemed to be self-financing and pay the lot. And if you check what the care homes in your area charge per week, 'the lot' is indeed a lot, believe me. You should be prepared to pay up to £1,000 per week and more, I kid you not.

The local assessment team will want to have sight of the relevant bank accounts, investments and the like, so I urge you to discover what it is that they require. Check what details of current and deposit accounts they will be asking for, and get hold of copies of the statements relating to those accounts.

This can take some time and effort, so don't wait until someone comes asking for them. For investments, properties and other assets, see their website for details.

I also urge you, if your financial arrangements are the least bit complicated, to do what I did, namely, to write down for the assessors in the form of an extended memorandum a detailed description of which accounts are which and an explanation for any transactions which remotely look as if deprivation of assets might be involved.

One example in our case was a largish transfer from one of my wife's deposit accounts a year or so before, which was part of a payment we had agreed to fund jointly for internal rebuilding and various other work.

There's one other issue which you should be aware of. If you are resident in England and Wales, you can ask the relevant POA provider for an access code which will enable officialdom to, er, access the POA online.

Unfortunately, this feature is not available in Scotland, and at the time of writing the Office of the Public Guardian tells me that there are no immediate plans for providing it, so you will have to ask what format will be acceptable to the people who require sight of the POA.

One other practical matter you should be prepared in advance to confront is the plethora of TLAs, as the Americans call them, which are devised by the professionals. TLA stands for Three Letter Acronyms like FBI, CIA, ATF, and so forth, but there are plenty of acronyms surrounding care out there which have three or more components.

We have already met OMG, BTW, POA and UTI, but that is just the tip of the iceberg. I would urge you to ask for an explanation if you do not understand a medical term or acronym which swims into view. BTW, if you are not computer-savvy, means By The Way, and the other TLA for texters which I treated you to earlier, OMG, stands for Oh My God.

This language barrier raised by in-house jargon comes to the fore in those formal meetings about the carer, with consultants, nurses, professional carers, mental health and social workers milling about in abundance. If you don't understand a word or phrase, do speak out and don't be too embarrassed to do so.

If it's any consolation, I have often discovered that many others round the table, professionals included, sigh with relief when I raise my head above the parapet to enquire about some inscrutable TLA or medical term. Some of the professionals too can be baffled, but not bold enough to show up their lack of knowledge.

One of my biggest areas for incomprehension is the inscrutable names for much of the medication, and also the differences between milligramme, centigramme and the rest. At least the situation is not quite as bad as when I once asked in a local DIY shop for a yard's length of a plank of wood.

I was told in no uncertain terms that we all work with the metrical system now. OK, I responded, duly humbled,

I'll have a metre length. Fine, said the shop assistant, and could you tell me if you want it half an inch thick and three quarters wide. Words fail me.

Chapter three – Being the main carer

One of the least recognised strains on the unpaid carer is the fact that he or she has to acquire the ability to switch roles seamlessly day or night.

It was recently explained to me by a specialist nurse in urology, with whom I had an appointment for reasons too embarrassing to detail here. He was describing how he coped with patients in circumstances which were uniquely private, to say the least, which was to detach himself from them and deal with each one as a 'mechanical body' requiring the technical skilled ability and expertise he had acquired, and when the consultation was over, he would switch off from that patient to allow the next gentleman in line to appear for treatment.

It was no different from lifting the bonnet of a car to repair it, then going on to the next vehicle. You may recall the long-running American Vietnam War comedy series MASH (Mobile Army Surgical Hospital), where doctors up to their elbows in the bleeding bodies of young men cruelly wounded on the battlefield would chatter and joke as they worked. That was a prime example, not of cruel indifference, but of coping mechanisms in an almost impossibly challenging daily situation of life and death decisions.

The specialist urology nurse didn't infer that his own detachment in any way meant that he was dehumanising his work or disrespecting the patient, but he too needed to come to terms with the fact that he had to distance himself in order to maintain his own self-esteem and mental health.

One of our sons is a hospital consultant in oncology, and he has found it can be extremely challenging to meet patient after patient and inform them that they may die soon. By the same token, the carer has to be emotionally detached. Problem is, that when the relationship is with your wife, as in my case, with whom you are the exact opposite of detached, things can get very tricky. I had a go at being professional and unemotional, though, and it sort of worked.

But I had also tackled the issue previously in a slightly different way which might work for you. It was something I didn't know I had acquired until I found myself dealing with first my father's and then my mother's death and funeral twenty years and more ago.

I managed somehow to switch into what I later called automatic mode to deal with preparations and the like, as I did more recently when, for example, I had to cope with dressing and undressing, replacing lift-up incontinence wear or dealing with soiled bedsheets and more. Emotions and the rest, I discovered, can became actually turned off to allow me to cope with the practicalities of the situation.

The worsening Parkinsons had all come about so gradually that it just became a part of normality, but I did manage to adapt.

Others may have much more difficulty in doing so, partly dependent upon the nature of their relationship with the person they are caring for, partly on their own reticence to perform certain tasks which are way out of their comfort zone. Nobody said this was easy, and it won't get easier.

Without getting too scientific about it, it's important for us all to have a role in family life, at work and in society at large, or a mix of fairly clearly defined roles. It helps us to establish who we are and what we do, and also how we think about ourselves.

The trouble about being a carer is that you have to juggle two mutually conflicting roles simultaneously, or alternate rapidly between them. And, as I have indicated, there couldn't be anything more polarised than a loving relationship on the one hand and a detached and skilled caring one on the other.

There's another important issue which kind of fits in here, and that is the question of your expertise as a carer in the awesome presence of consultants and others who have had the benefit of years of training and experience in Parkinsons, dementia and related ailments.

In your defence, you should point out to them that this is the first time you have encountered this particular situation and are having to make it up as you go along.

By contrast, the professionals deal with similar patients on a daily basis and take a lot as said which we cannot be expected to be aware of. On the other hand, even though you are flying by the seat of your pants, so to speak, you do accumulate and exploit a very great deal of other expertise along the way.

This is a key factor, which the professionals can tend to overlook. You too are an expert – in the person you're caring for as a human being, and this can make a crucial contribution to guiding their attitude and which should be fed into their decision-making procedures. So my advice is that you should not be overawed by anyone. Ever. Speak up.

You have your rightful place in the consultation process as well as in the key decisions taken. Remember, if you are too timid to challenge a point or demand that something should be better explained, of course you cannot be knocked back. But if you don't pluck up the courage to do so, you will never succeed in making any positive contribution to the best proper care.

Let me illustrate this with a meeting between the hospital consultant, a legal adviser, Rusalka, her son and daughter, and nurses and a roomful of other relevant professionals. Rusalka had recently been sectioned under the Mental Health Act for reasons which made my blood boil.

They informed me that even in her psychotic state, when she demanded to be released from hospital, sectioning was the only route they could take to force her to stay, because she had 'human rights' which tend to demand attention at the most inconvenient of moments in healthcare. Then, on top of that, the sectioning can only be valid for fourteen days, after which a serious legal process had to be undergone to retain her further in the hospital.

That was what the meeting was now about. I faced a

huge dilemma. Rusalka had been an in-patient for just six weeks, a blink of the eye in mental health terms, but she was desperately unhappy in the hospital, although it was a newish building where the individual rooms were not far short of Premier Inn quality. (Other hotels are available.) She was demanding to be released, and this is what the meeting centred on.

So I was faced with a decision: either to allow the legal eagles to do their thing and compel her to stay for a longer period, or to speak out and take the risk of withdrawing her from the hospital, which I yearned to do, and cope with her over an extended period of recovery. I knew the latter option could be challenging, to put it mildly, but I drew on my thirty-odd years expertise in knowing my wife and her personality, and so I took the plunge.

I did insist, though, on having some enhanced carer support which was willingly given, so I agreed to drive her home and face the music. I was rather glad that I did, mainly in retrospect.

Also, I have good reason to believe that the medics were just a tiny bit relieved by my excessive optimism and determination, since they were not convinced that an extended stay in hospital would greatly advance her treatment.

After a couple of weeks of really tricky interactions with her, she gradually emerged back into the land of the living, so to speak, and the decision I made did indeed grant her an extended period of time out of institutional care. We both emerged bloody but unbowed. If I had not piped up and put forward my case she may well still have been in hospital.

All this decision-making was underpinned by the concept of care in the community for mental health patients (which we had ironically both championed many years ago), but I guess that if I had not intervened, I could otherwise have been steamrollered into a situation where she became institutionalised at far too early a stage in the gathering severity of her illness. To borrow another acronym beloved of Americans, it was a case of ODTAA. One Damned Thing After Another.

Chapter four – Help!

I turn now to a topic which is much neglected but of considerable practical importance: What happens if the person you're caring for has a fall or other accident and you are not right next to them to assist?

Here's a tale that ought to be true, but unfortunately it isn't. NASA was busily blasting Americans into space in the Apollo missions when they came up against a big problem. The ink pens which they were using wouldn't write in zero gravity, so they spent millions of dollars of tax payers' money on trying to find a substitute which did function properly, until one fine day the Russians offered to let them try out the item of equipment they employed themselves, namely, a pencil.

So we all duly fall about laughing at the pen-pushers (appropriate term, that) keenly avoiding the screamingly obvious and rushing headlong up the nearest and most expensive blind alley. Except, there is just one inconvenient truth which spoils a perfectly good story. It isn't true.

You will find the full details of what really happened online in a *Scientific American* article published on 20 December, 2006, which underlines the consideration that pencils (a) could be hazardous in space, with bits of lead and sharp fragments of wood floating round the capsule and (b) they were a fire hazard, and after the disastrous conflagration of Apollo 1 during launchpad testing they did not want that repeating.

It seems that in the end NASA did develop a working pen, or rather a commercial company did so for them, and the resulting product was also used by the Russians.

At which point, you may be asking yourself what on earth this has to do with helping someone who experiences an emergency of some kind when they are out of immediate contact with the carer. In my wife's case, that would usually involve having a fall as a result of Parkinsons causing dizziness and lack of balance.

Now we get to the heart of the matter. What is the best means of managing this situation? Do you need a high-tech pen or a basic pencil? Or both? In answering the question, I am going to get into all kinds of trouble with local authorities in the answer to the problem I encountered. But it is an issue which sorely needs to be addressed head on.

The approach I was offered was called the community alarm. This system is long in the tooth and pretty clunky, and consists of a largish button worn either on the wrist or round the neck. A unit sits monitoring the button. Press the alarm and it dials up central control and a voice asks if the user is OK, and if not, what help is needed. It's at this point that the first issue arises.

The main unit is located on a sideboard next to the landline input to the house. Let's assume that the person you're caring for is lying on the floor of a bedroom at the other end of the house, having slipped and done an unknown amount of damage to themselves. This means that the there is no way of communicating the nature of the problem to the monitoring controller which the local authority had installed, or responding that they have inadvertently pressed the button by mistake, which can happen, believe me.

In a case where the person who has had an accident is within shouting distance of the control box, what happens next if a callout is required? The next assumption is that a vehicle with trained responders is sitting within reasonable distance of the emergency caller.

The next supposition is that the responders can gain access to the house when they get there. All that depends on the system not being offline because of a power cut, a not infrequent occurrence here out in the sticks, and a key safe to which they know the code, and into which the last carer to use it has remembered to return the key. If an ambulance is needed, valuable time has been wasted in the process.

No system will work perfectly all the time, as with every kind of accident or other request for assistance. Life is like that, but we should do everything reasonable to maximise the likelihood of a prompt response to any call for help.

I urge you to think long and hard about taking the appropriate precautions and to beware of local authority workers bearing gifts in the form of community alarms. I politely agreed to have one fitted, because Health and Safety, bless it, insisted on it being installed if they are to employ care workers attending the home. It lay quietly there, unused, until my wife entered the care home, at which point

I courteously requested that the offending equipment should be taken away.

I am not going to presume to tell you what precise steps you should take in emergency situations, simply to invite you to follow basic principles for your own security and peace of mind, and also that of the person you're caring for. Please remember two things at this point: first, it is way beyond the scope of this book to test and evaluate all the devices on the market, and, secondly, the technology is constantly evolving at a breakneck pace and it is for you to keep up to speed with those changes.

If you have an Alexa device or similar, for example, a whole range of options are available for home security and personal protection, and they keep evolving merrily away. Many of these are rolled out first in the USA and only later in other countries. Remember that Alexa or her equivalent is also available on mobile phones and other platforms.

Then there is a simple wristband I noticed online called Buddi which incorporates a motion sensor so that it can determine whether someone is falling, and it then informs your mobile phone of the potential accident. That is just one option amongst many which may be worth considering.

Now I will get into more trouble, this time with the sellers of smart phones. If you cannot or will not afford to dish out the grandkids' inheritance on a mobile phone, do scour the market for a less expensive option which still does all the fancy stuff of SMS, taking high resolution pictures, going on line, running apps and so forth. Oh, yes, and it allows you to make and receive telephone calls. My point is that I was in this situation and managed to purchase a new phone with all those features plus a huge screen for less than a hundred pounds.

So spend some time exploring the options before making your choice, remembering that in this day and age technology is cheap and you do not have to stay committed to one particular solution.

Remember too that the person you're caring for is becoming increasingly fragile and forgetful, and will become increasingly so, and as a result you should make the response to an emergency, real or imagined, as straightforward as possible.

Also, when you arrive on scene, as they say, take a few moments to assess the situation. I have got into terrible bother more than once by telling my wife that, no, her fall is not serious and that there is no need to call the Air Ambulance to deal with her situation. Besides, the farmer across the road would not take kindly to his winter wheat being crushed and trampled in the process.

A hysterical and disproportionate reaction to a minor tumble, for example, is not unusual, and time spent comforting and assuring the person you're caring for that no bones are broken and bruising will be minor or undetectable is well worth the effort.

The options I decided on, starting out in the days before most of the technology I have described came on to the market, were to ensure, as far as it was possible, that her mobile phone was charged and with her at all times. She used a rollator to facilitate her mobility round the house, so it was necessary to ensure that the phone was in a pocket of the machine. As an aside, if you are considering a rollator, do go for one with a seat which enables them to rest and catch their breath and also helps them to clamber back up in the event of a fall.

Any solution to this problem of an alarm should have as few moving parts as possible. The question also arose as to what would happen if in the heat of the moment the person you're caring for forgot how to operate the phone or had not even remembered to carry it with them, and it is at this point (no pun intended) that the pencil solution came into my mind.

I'm not a serious film buff, but one movie which really attracted me when I was nowt but a lad, as they say in Yorkshire, was *Genevieve*, a comedy based on the London to Brighton run for vintage cars. Apart from the catchy harmonica tune, the one sound which stuck in my mind was the sharp call of the old car horn, a simple device which was very strident and consisted of a rubber squeezable ball and a trumpet-shaped amplifier which could be heard for miles around. It sounded like a lady elephant in the pangs of childbirth. It also required zero electricity and connectivity to work. Nor did it need batteries. That is a low-tech pencil solution to the problem.

I bought a handful of the bicycle version and fixed one of them to the rollator. Strategically located, they could easily be audible from one end of the house to the other, and served very well in the cause of emergency communications. It was the simplest form of technology (if it even deserved the term), but it worked, and more importantly, it functioned in just about any crisis situation, perceived or real, even during a power cut.

Let's see if I can sum up from these brief excursions into the bells and whistles, so to speak, of sounding the alarm. Here are my do's and don't's for exploring solutions to emergency issues:

(1) Remember the carer first and foremost. Design your options around their needs, weaknesses and capabilities, and do not work outwards from the technology. Ever.

(2) Use the minimum possible technological level to achieve your desired result.

(3) Adapt existing technology, like a mobile phone or Alexa, rather than a scratch-built new complex alternative, in which you may well find that design gets in the way of function, and fancy features obscure the intention.

(4) Never, repeat, never rely on just one option. Have at least two or more alternatives ready to be

called on. There is no point, for example, in just having an emergency button stuck halfway up a wall if it can't be reached from the prone position.

(5) Be flexible and adaptable. The technology you use today will soon be past its sell-by date, so be prepared to explore a new or up-to-date alternative.

(6) Involve the person you're caring for at all levels of acquiring and installing solutions. Never lose sight of the fact that the only reason you are considering all this is the safety and well-being of the person you're caring for, not your convenience or that of others.

Remember, too, that the best of equipment is no use if it isn't being monitored or can't be accessed. And to use another of those US acronyms, KISS. Keep It Simple, Stupid. (Not you, of course.)

Here's a cautionary tale to end with. A few years back, a product came on to the market which claimed to solve security issues caused by callers in your absence from the home, namely, a doorbell incorporating a video camera which could dial up your mobile phone and allow you to talk to the delivery driver or debt collector or whoever.

To put it politely, these gizmos were sold at a premium price. As a result, a booming trade built up amongst the criminal fraternity who would no longer bother to break into the property in order to steal, they simply removed the video doorbell device itself and sold that on. And that rather defeats the object of the exercise.

Chapter five – The trivial round, the common task

All too often little attention was paid in the past to the huge changes which happen to your life when retirement occurs. This was probably due to the fact that not many people could enjoy an extended period in retirement, the lower life expectancy of past times saw to that. Now, however, it is becoming a serious issue, as retirement has now morphed into the beginning of a new era in life.

It has even grown not one, but two names: The Third Age (65-80) and The Fourth Age (80 plus). By the way, the title of this chapter was borrowed from John Keble's hymn 'New Every Morning Is the Love'.

When someone is first introduced at a gathering of any kind, regardless of the context, the first two questions addressed to them will almost inevitably be: What is your name and what do you do? In other words, the career path you are following is high up on the agenda of interests on the part of the others present.

Our work forms a key aspect of ourselves as people, and being employed is not simply a means of putting food on the table, it also helps to define who we are and how we occupy a considerable part of our time.

When these questions are posed, listen to the silence when you have to say: 'I'm retired now.' The unspoken response is: that's not a job, it's pretty well as bad as confessing 'I'm unemployed,' or the much nicer euphemism which professional actors use: 'I'm resting at the moment.'

As you can guess, I am labouring the point that 'retirement' can be seen as a negative – a huge great hole which has been created in your life and you have somehow to fill it.

You may have seen the film *The Full Monty* – and if you haven't, do so, and not just for the cheeky (I use the word advisedly) bit at the end. It's a compassionate account of a group of working men who lost their jobs and decide to become male strippers. Their former supervisor is also thrown out of work, but it only becomes obvious to his wife when the bailiffs arrive to repossess the television.

He has been sallying forth in his smart suit and tie every day plus briefcase to pretend that everything is normal, because that was the only way he could cope with the situation without completely forfeiting his self-esteem and dignity. His role in the film is acted to perfection and very poignantly.

It is some decades now since employers began to take preparing their workforce for retirement seriously, but that does not help the legions of self-employed, who face exactly the same difficulties of adjustment without the comfort blanket of a company, large or small.

Deposited at home all day, the husband might be sitting in his chair, getting under the wife's feet as she goes about hoovering, preparing the dinner and doing the washing.

You can imagine the marital strife that can flare up in

such circumstances. And I have still left out one possible response to that second question posed when people meet for the first time.

What if you reply when asked what you do: 'I'm a full-time carer.' That causes a mumble of sympathetic responses with people staring in an embarrassed fashion into their wine glasses. An emergency change of subject is activated. And to be a carer *and* retired is a double whammy.

All right, then, enough of negativity. The point I'm struggling to arrive at is that you may be a full-timer carer, but you should not be embarrassed by the fact. It is a role which is essential in holding the social fabric together, not to mention the fact that carers are saving the country vast sums of money. However, it must not define all that you are. In order to remain a fully rounded person, it's essential to be able to switch off, to enjoy 'you time', which I am now going to explore in some detail.

First, my own situation, as this is a personal story. As an author and academic, I am fortunate in being largely self-motivated and a major chunk of the job consisted of working on my own, researching and writing. In addition, I also found myself becoming a part-time journalist as well as a writer, publisher and later a computer programmer designing educational software.

So when I was cut loose and took early retirement, I could actually, as they say in the music business, segue seamlessly into my new situation and continue to be involved in those activities that kept me busy in the workplace.

In academia, though, the better you get at your job as lecturer and gain recognition, the higher you are promoted, the less research and teaching you are able to do, until you get to being professor and head of department, when you are spending a very large percentage of your time being an administrator and manager, and the actual research and teaching can tend to become largely squeezed out of the picture. So retirement can arrive as a blessed relief from chairing meetings and dictating and signing letters and student report cards.

However, I very much sympathise with the many of you for whom work does not offer such opportunities, and that can cause considerable problems when you leave the workplace and find yourself at a loose end.

You may take up something like an Open University course, but that is, as they say, no walk in the park. If you are better with your hands than your head, DIY can be a consolation, but don't take a wrecking ball to the house and create havoc in the process.

Hobbies and pastimes from your workaday life should not be cast aside: if you play golf or engage in some other sporting activity, or if you are a member of a club, organisation, or charitable group, find ways of keeping those activities alive.

However, in the later stages of caring, you will need to

bring in someone to keep an eye on the person you're caring for while you are out of the house, as they may be otherwise in danger of hurting themselves, doing damage, or experiencing a fall and then being unable to stand up under their own steam.

Do not become a couch potato. I must confess I am guilty as charged, as I hate exercise. I find the whole business tedious, and I have discovered that it just makes me tired. And I ache, too.

My excuse is that there is a substantial amount of exercise involved in simply being a carer, just going back and forward from one end of the house to the other to perform all the tasks which form part of my role. I worked out that from the main bedroom to the sitting room was just under forty steps, and I was going to call this book 'The thirty-nine Steps', but I am reliably informed that it has already been used.

Here comes another piece of advice which I urge you to follow. Keep to a regular routine. Do not let your days become an uncontrolled mess of activities or, more likely, inactivity. As for eating, I always ensure that I prepare and consume one proper meal per day, although I don't count the calories or ensure I have five a day of whatever I am supposed to by the food fascists.

I tend not to eat carbohydrates and proteins, I just eat food. I have discovered, however, that purely by chance I am not completely devoid of nutritional sense, as I always have a large bowlful of wholegrain muesli for breakfast from a well-known manufacturer, although there are some days, after a sleepless night, when it tastes like the discarded sweepings from a mountain pathway.

I'm not sure where to put this next piece of advice, so I'll add it in here, even though in many cases I'm teaching grandmothers to suck eggs. Nowadays, one significant means of support for a retired carer which you may well not have considered is that of shopping online rather than actually venturing out to the high street or local mall.

This can be a challenge if you are worried about leaving someone alone in the house. I am referring here principally to what they call in Scotland 'doing the messages', which refers to groceries and other everyday household requirements.

Getting the supplies brought to you, especially the heavy stuff like potatoes and cans and bottles and more, is a considerable saver of time and effort. And at the time of writing, new forms of such shopping are now gradually emerging, with companies taking up the notion of providing almost instant deliveries.

Send in your order, and it is brought to you with a modest charge within hours rather than days. At the time of writing, these facilities are mainly available in the large conurbations, but watch this space.

Whether or not in the medium term drones will become a serious contender in this market, I don't know. The prospect of the airspace being cluttered with autonomous model aeroplanes colliding and falling out of the sky with my groceries on board doesn't sound too brilliant.

Also, it is too easy to become a recluse (at which point I add a note to self: try harder not to be). Do not stay in the house or flat day after day. If you are fortunate enough to have a garden, take a regular walk around and pull up a few weeds. If you are in an apartment, find a nearby park for your wanderings.

And now I turn to a topic which for me was rather contentious, but I know that it can be extremely helpful and a necessary part of long-term caring.

Chapter six – Respite

You may find yourself under less than gentle pressure from your social worker – or CMHT if you are involved with them – to take some time to yourself, so that you can recharge your batteries (to coin a phrase). It has become a kind of panacea for the negative aspects of caring, but I am not entirely convinced of its merits.

Respite can assume several forms. Let's deal first with the notion of respite for the carer, in which you are invited to take some days off, or go to sessions for groups of carers.

To step entirely out of character and become facetious for a moment, my distaste knows no bounds for confessional meetings, almost like AA gatherings, where everyone sits round in a circle (using first names only – 'My name is Jim', 'Hello Jim') and random victims are persuaded thereafter to ventilate their problems in public and hold forth about their emotions, or that dreadful mental health buzzword 'issues'.

It reminds me of the young lady who was not exactly eager in her response to the advances of some pimpled youth who one evening tried to invite her round to his place. She responded with the immortal put-down: 'I'd rather dive naked into a vat of warm giraffe vomit.' I'd go along with that. As long as it's warm.

However, some folk may actually enjoy exposing their souls in public. If that suits you, all power to your elbow.

But, as I have already emphasised, this is not a situation

where a verbal purgative necessarily results in a long-term positive outcome. It may just clear the air for a while, and I suspect the greatest benefit of such gatherings is being able to chat with people before and after the main event.

Despite that, however much we may discuss and expand on our experiences, it does not change the fundamentals of our situation one jot. You may briefly feel a little better for so doing, but when you get back home, you are confronted with the same situation as when you left.

Also, the person you're caring for may not be too overjoyed with the prospect of going out for day care to provide the carer with a breathing space. My wife has a similar aversion to joining a jolly group playing Bingo (an anagram, I like to point out, of Big No) or sitting round with the TV welded on to ITV3.

The second kind of support can come from professional carers whom you either fund directly or though the agency of the local authority. I arranged for carers to give her a twice-weekly shower, and to help dress her and deal with her medication. That gave me short breaks during the day, and allowed her to gossip with her carers.

Check carefully any funding issues with the powers that be. These interventions are invaluable, but the downside can be that of staff turnover. It is unsettling for the person you're caring for to be constantly confronted with unfamiliar faces whom you have to train into dealing with their tasks and the specific requirements of their client.

My real problem with respite of more than a day for either of us would be that if I was long absent from my wife, I'd spend all the time fretting about her, particularly when she got to the stage of accidentally doing harm to herself with a needle, knife or pair of scissors, or setting the house on fire, which nearly happened on one occasion. Some respite that would be. (Come home to a real fire, as the advert used to say.)

I wasn't convinced either that having the person you're caring for take a fortnight out to give me a break would have the desired effect. We actually tried it, but for a variety of reasons it didn't work too well.

Don't be too put off by my reservations, which are mostly specific to our situation and people involved, but do give it a go, recognising that the fortnight (a week is too short for someone to become acclimatised to a care home environment) could well become a prelude to a permanent stay.

Now I take a look at one of the least pleasant aspects of Parkinsons as it increases its hold.

Chapter seven – The psychotic episode

One fine day you may find yourself in a crisis situation at home in which the person you are caring for undergoes an acute psychotic episode. Not everyone has to confront that undesirable prospect, but it is one of the less pleasant side-effects of Parkinsons. Here are some words of advice and, I hope, comfort for carers who find themselves in that position.

To begin with, it can happen out of a clear blue sky, or there may be advance signs over an extended period that something is becoming seriously amiss. If it appears without apparent warning, it will be necessary for your doctor to check for the presence of a UTI (Urinary Tract Infection). Parkinsons patients are particularly prone to UTIs. Once that has been treated, the problem should begin to abate.

As the main carer, you may otherwise notice gradually increased anxiety, inwardness, odd or compulsive behaviour, auditory or visual hallucinations, or any combination of these. This is indicative that the more worrying kind of psychotic episode may be in the offing.

In addition, there seems to be some inbuilt law of nature which states that most mental health crises arise at around five in the afternoon on a Friday, just after staff have gone home and the weekend looms.

The worst part is going to visit to the psychiatric hospital, if things get that serious, and being violently confronted by someone you hardly recognise. One of the problems which is apparently common for patients in that situation (fat consolation that is) is for the carer to be accused of all manner of sexual antics in their absence, as I indicated earlier.

Personality changes are also par for the course. You should hope and believe this is something temporary, which will not become permanent when the patient leaves hospital.

Paranoia leaves a long trail behind it, and it may take weeks or longer for the distorted perceptions it generates to dissipate, if they do disappear altogether, that is. In addition, auditory and visual hallucinations can persist, and they can be particularly concerning when the patient is genuinely convinced that they are not making them up.

As a non-medic, I can only write from my own experience, but it appears to be true that such unwelcome episodes accelerate the progress of the illness. It seems in the case of Parkinsons that once an additional step in a downwards direction has taken place, there is no way that the juggernaut can be persuaded to go into reverse, so to speak.

On the contrary, it just goes faster. This, as I have said before, is a one-way trip and there is no way of engaging reverse gear and taking one or more paces back.

You can hope for the best, but t could well be a foretaste of things to come. I cannot offer any consolation about that. This 'dreadful illness', as the professionals call it, can and does result in pretty unpleasant consequences.

Chapter eight – Keeping your head above water

I turn now to some practical issues which arise when the person you've been caring for full-time enters a care home, and I begin with some general advice about coping with officialdom, which you will have to do when the move takes place and thereafter.

This can be quite a challenge if you are not familiar with such folk, and you are confronted with a flurry of phone calls and suchlike to make at a time when you are feeling pretty vulnerable and miserable.

One of the most tiresome six words in the English language must be those you hear when you are put on hold after navigating your way through a maze of menus from a call centre, namely, 'Your call is valuable to us'. Do not get wound up and start shouting at people.

It can be frustrating to have to deal with call centre staff whose lives are driven by the rulebook rather than loving interactions, but, to drag up the obsolete phrase, 'Softly, softly, catchee monkey'. In other words do not allow yourself to become upset and wrathful.

I advise this in particular when you come up against a brick wall when you use phrases like 'I am calling on behalf of...', which instantly evokes the response that you should summon the person you are calling on behalf of to the phone so that they can confirm that you are indeed allowed to speak for them.

Leaving on one side the fact that you could recruit your next door neighbour to act the part of the person you've been caring for, rather like offering a photo of yourself as proof of your identity, the next obstacle is that you tell the voice at the other end of the line that you have a POA. The response then, of course, is that they must have sight of it before you can proceed. Just count up to ten and meekly oblige.

Let the rules of others not cause you to rush screaming out into the street. My self-restraint knows no bounds when the delivery driver calls with a large boxful of my latest favourite tipple, zero alcohol Guinness, and insists on recording on his phone my date of birth, even though it is fairly obvious just by observing me that I am hardly some illiterate underage alcoholic youth out to drink themselves to death.

And don't get me started on our local superstore which like others can only deliver alcohol free beverages within the same hours as are permitted by their more potent companions. Every little helps, as they say.

The next topic I want to turn to may not fit in here comfortably (or anywhere else for that matter), but it's something which has caused me considerable disquiet and which I want to share with you, together with my own views on the matter.

It was kick-started by a throwaway remark made to me by a lady, who shall remain anonymous, which I think was intended to be helpful, but which I found pretty hurtful and, I suspect, tinged with just the tiniest little amount of envy.

She was talking about the trials and tribulations of a carer who has to witness someone entering a care or nursing home, when she added, 'Of course, you don't want to carry on rattling around in that great big house of yours.'

Her information about our residence must have been anecdotal, unless she had snuck in through the keyhole and taken a good look round, but there are a couple of assertions here which seriously need picking apart.

First up is the implication that the carer would surely not want to continue living in the same house, flat or whatever, as you have dwelt in together for a good few years. Too many memories for comfort would surely be swirling around you.

Implication number two is a touch more sinister, and that is the notion that anything more than a cramped sheltered flat with a bedsit, a small-screen telly and a microwave is somehow morally tainted, a kind of bed blocking, cruelly preventing the next generation and their offspring from taking over the 'unused' space to build their own little or not so little nest.

Let me consider these matters one at a time. The first is a quite serious concern that living amongst the cherished ghosts of the past imposes yet another burden on the absentee carer, which can readily be resolved by simply moving house and downsizing. The financial advantages could also be considerable. These are arguments which need careful consideration on your part.

Starting with the alleged trauma of continuing to live in the same house as you both lived before, I am sure that not everyone will be of the same opinion. This is a decision for you alone to make. Do not let yourself become pressurised into making a hasty decision by the views of others who are not in the same situation as yourself. Take your time and consider all the implications.

I can only put forward my own reaction to the new situation. My wife and I lived happily in this house for a very long time, nearly forty years, bringing up her two children in their teenage years and accumulating quite a lot of memories then and thereafter.

The house also grew during our time here. When we moved in, it was just about derelict, a cottage a hundred and fifty years old plus a nearly finished extension of three bedrooms and a bathroom. And a quarter of an acre of garden, also derelict.

Now it boasts an additional large upstairs study cum library and a host of other improvements, large and small. Far more important than that is the fact that we had expended a great deal of money and effort on making the house user friendly for my wife as her mobility decreased and her needs went in the opposite direction.

Which means that, although she no longer lives here, our living space is ready for the time when I become wheelchair dependent and need home care. That's one solid reason for continuing to live here.

The downside is that it is quite expensive to run and that might tempt the occupant to consider moving. Think first, though, of alternatives. I presume that lifetime mortgages can still be arranged in cases where the house is jointly owned and one of the owners is in full-time care, but that and other considerations need careful thought and expert advice.

If the argument raises its ugly head that you must leave as much money to the children as you can, remember that you have your own difficult life to lead right now. I shall probably get boiled in oil for saying this, but I am often tempted to ask what posterity has ever done for me.

I know this may be contentious, but you really must consider yourself and how to make the rest of your life as comfortable and mentally stable as possible. If the children challenge this I would begin to wonder about their prime motivation.

I still haven't taken account of the emotional and psychological implications of continuing to reside in a home which is filled with memories of a dearly-loved wife who is no longer living there. In my own case, after a couple of months flying solo, so to speak, I have no doubt that staying in the house has been the right decision for me. I find it oddly comforting to walk amongst the signs of her past presence all the time.

For me, it would in addition be far too challenging to up

sticks and move into unfamiliar accommodation which I would have to repurpose just for myself. It would be a barren place without memories, too. And do think hard about the amount of physical effort involved in such work.

Your advancing years may not be compatible with slapping on new wallpaper, and there may be considerable expense involved in calling upon the local electrician, carpenter, plumber, decorator and others to carry out necessary alterations and improvements.

Living on here is rather like looking through all those old pre-smartphone photographs of family life and more. They serve to keep memories alive and, of course they may frequently be sad rather than cheerful, but as the lady in the ballad sang, 'I never promised you a rose garden' (the songbird was Lynn Anderson). To become detached from my past would almost certainly be far more painful than accepting and embracing it.

Downsizing would also be seriously challenging in the choices I would have to make of what stuff to get rid of, particularly those possessions which my wife gathered together over the years.

The office in which I am keying in these words just now, for example, contains a large amount of shelving groaning with books, less than half of which are mine, the rest are a myriad of cookery guides which Rusalka accumulated, many plucked from the shelves of the local charity shops.

The fitted wardrobe up here is cluttered with her

numerous hats and handbags, and there are legions of shoes lying largely unused there and throughout the various rooms and cupboards of the house, so many in fact that I have commented on more than one occasion that I had no idea that I had married a centipede. Make that a millipede. 'So many shoes, so little time,' seems to have been her mantra.

There is another person apart from yourself in this situation who hardly gets a mention when the question of moving house comes up for consideration, and that of course is my wife herself, now in her nursing home.

When I visit her, she often fondly mentions our home and garden, because it forms part of her past, too, and for her to have to face the fact that it no longer exists, as it were, would be very disturbing indeed for her.

One final obstacle to take into account is the fact that moving house constitutes one of the most traumatic and challenging self-inflicted life experiences you can put yourself through, and if, like me, you are well past your allotted three score years and ten, it can be an experience too far.

In all these matters, my advice would be to look very long and hard indeed before you leap, to take as much time you need in order to think through the implications of your options, and to remember above all that your choices should be driven not simply by practical considerations but also by the very significant emotional challenges involved.

One final point on accommodation: do not allow yourself to become pressurised into making the wrong decision by those who would have you move because it is somehow 'wrong' or 'selfish' to live in accommodation which they in their wisdom deem to be too large for one individual. My response to the lady who started all this off is that I rather like to rattle around and will continue to rattle for so long as I can manage to do so. The alternative would be too distressful for me to bear.

The last part of this chapter on managing as an absentee carer is a little bit on the delicate side, so I will tread warily.

Let me begin by telling you what happened to me one morning shortly after Rusalka was found a permanent place in a nursing home. I needed a haircut, so I called in on the barber's in town, which is run by a very compassionate lady who asked me each time I turned up how my wife was and how I was coping. She put the usual question as I arrived and I told her rather shakily that Rusalka was now in residential care.

Her spontaneous reaction was to come up to me and give me a big hug, offering me words of comfort at the same time. I must admit I was surprised, but very touched (literally). After the haircut, I walked across in the sunshine towards a nearby café, where a small group of locals were enjoying coffee and a gossip under the pavement sunshades.

Two of the ladies I knew quite well, as they were members of the same association as Rusalka and myself, and I went across to say hello. They too asked me about Rusalka and were shocked to hear of her decline and placement in a care home. In turn, each of them got up, hugged me and offered me their sympathies.

Those two incidents helped me to formulate how I am going to approach the delicate subject of intimacy. It occurred to me after much soul-searching that I was getting two distinct topics muddled up in my head, namely, the need for physical contact on the one hand, and sexuality on the other.

The reaction of these kind ladies to my distress was to offer physical contact and genuine warmth, and I was greatly moved by it, as I recognised that this was what I had been lacking and, with the exception of visits two or three times a week, would continue to miss with my wife being no longer at home with me.

The instinctive offering of physical contact as a sign of compassion and support was most welcome, but it also painfully highlighted a serious issue for absentee carers which they would have to come to terms with. Loneliness will inevitably be added to the mix of other disagreeable feelings and emotions which present themselves.

It is a tragedy that in the current climate, some woke folk might be tempted to regard all this touchy-feely stuff as unwanted sexual contact, and to seek to string the lot of us up in the nearby town on adjacent lampposts as additional ornaments to the Christmas decorations which have been stuck there all year, due to lockdown. After, that is, grovelling apologies were made on Facebook and the like.

My generation as a whole will have none of such nonsense, and we do recognise like most people that human contact, from babyhood upwards, is a key need for each and every one of us.

And tragically, that need is tied irrevocably to the one person in your life who is slipping away from you because of the increasing symptoms of Parkinsons and more. Others can assist in alleviating the distress, but it will not simply melt away. It is a painful additional burden we all have to bear.

Other more challenging causes for your distress can occur, and I hesitantly put forward one of my own. I emphasise elsewhere the fact that memories of the good times together cannot be erased, but one unfortunate side effect has recently occurred to me as part of the 'slippery slope' of this book's title, namely, that the hard years of being a full-time carer can tend to blur the recollection of those good times and render them less powerful and less acutely felt.

It's not that I have forgotten them at all, it's simply that the emotional intensity of being a full-time carer has somehow dimmed those memories and rendered them more distant, and that depresses me greatly.

From all I have been saying, it will be clear to you that there is little to be done to mitigate the deep sadness and sense of loss this lack of contact can bring. Bite the bullet and learn to come to terms with it is the only suggestion I can offer. But here comes one idea to help chase the demons away, even though it is just temporary.

This appears at first sight to be a flippant piece of advice, but I mean it in all earnestness. If you are going through a particularly bleak and isolated time, remember that nothing cheers you up more than a good laugh. It is somehow cathartic and helps to mitigate those miserable emotions swirling around inside you.

It is in no way disrespectful to the person you've cared for or their condition to employ this means of lightening your load. Somewhere in a dusty corner of your brains, all of you have a collection of comic incidents and radio or TV programmes which have brought you to tears, in a nice way. Dig them out (YouTube is a good resource) and see if they can help raise you from your understandable despair.

Here's a trio of dated and tasteless offerings from my own private collection. First, the Gerard Hoffnung Oxford Union address I mentioned earlier, and not just for the bricklayer and the letter to his boss. Look also for the Tyrolean landlady sequence, which contains the famous encouragement to potential visitors: 'There is a French widow in every bedroom.' YouTube has sound-only recordings of the Hoffnung.

Secondly, try out the famous self-questioning humourist Tony Hancock from the black and white TV days. A series called 'Hancock's Half Hour', including 'The Blood Donor', is well worth watching. Make sure you find the sound and vision version. In sound only, enjoy the destruction of international relations with Japan in 'The Radio Ham'.

You'll have to drag the third example out of me, but OK, I yield. Here goes with a demolition of my reputation as an earnest and serious-minded academic. It's the trailer for the children's cartoon film *Ice Age*. Again, YouTube has it, but make sure you find the excerpt with 'acorn trouble' as its subject. I defy anyone to keep a straight face watching that.

If those don't make you feel a touch better, at least for a while, you have no soul. Your favourites may well differ from mine, but the old cliché about laughter being the best medicine is true. Sometimes it's the only medication available. As a footnote to all this, I should stress that of course music can also have a very important cathartic role to play when you are feeling particularly low.

If you are a pop fan, opt for something uplifting like an Abba singalong; if your tastes are more classical, try the complete score of *The Gondoliers* by Gilbert and Sullivan, or the final movement of Saint-Saens's Organ Symphony.

Now I turn to the other matter which had become tangled up with physical contact in my muddled mind, namely, sexuality. You will not be surprised to hear that I propose to offer little or no personal advice in this area, for a number of good reasons.

Each of us is different in our reactions to the problems raised by Parkinsons, and they are compounded by the ageing process, which can cause reduced sex drive and cause issues like erectile dysfunction which intensify the situation.

In addition, for many people sexual matters are difficult to discuss and individuals require very different approaches and support. I also take the view that sexuality is an issue separate from Parkinsons, although the disease can exacerbate the challenges you may face.

I am only an expert in my own relations with Rusalka, and it is beyond my competence to try and offer general advice, especially because of the highly individual and sensitive nature of the issues involved.

So I am going to duck out of this debate, not least because the Michael J Fox foundation website has a page of such comprehensive information that I could not hope to offer that level of detail in its exploration of the subject. You will find the relevant page here:

https://www.michaeljfox.org/news/sexual-reproductive-health

There's another excellent report on the subject on the ilcuk.org.uk website. The link is rather long, so go to the main page and click on the magnifying glass and search for sexuality.

Finally, there is one additional point to make. Some of the medication used in Parkinsons, notably Ropinirole, can significantly increase sexual drive. I leave it to you to manage that problem. If, that is, you find it is a problem.

Chapter nine – Confronting the issues

Don't get angry about particular aspects of the condition of the person you care for. You should not espouse the foolish view that the professionals know nothing, since you have googled all the world's websites on the subject of Parkinsons and therefore know everything about it. Wrong.

You don't have knowledge, you have just facts, and quite a lot of competing facts at that. On top of that, you have not acquired the expertise to manage and assimilate all those facts into knowledge and use them wisely. Such expert behaviour is developed only after a long time and a great deal of study and practical experience.

Don't ever come to believe that Google empowers you to tell the experts what to think or do. I am not being deferential, far from it, as my wife and I many years ago challenged a hostile establishment of consultants for reasons I don't want to write about here, and we achieved a huge amount of progress in the way that carers in mental health were treated (badly, in those days, and kept out of the loop) both nationally in the UK, and in her trips and conference addresses across Europe, too.

I recognise, as you must too, that the general practitioner, the pharmacist, the consultant and the specialist nurse all have years of training behind them, and even more importantly, they possess more actual experience of our situation than we as individual carers can possibly acquire.

Disagreements can and will occur, as we rage against the

darkness closing in on their patient. My honest view is twofold: first, I believe that the vast majority of folk in those professions do their level best for the patient and their carer nowadays, and any mistakes they make in a difficult situation, like deciding on the appropriate level and nature of medication, tend to be better than the best we as lay people could manage.

In mental health, it is more often the case than not that interventions are taken, like increasing or changing medication, based on what the consultant will describe as 'making a judgment call'. In other words, dealing with mental health is more challenging than physical ailments in this respect.

It most emphatically does not signify that the medics are less competent. Frequently, medication in this area takes some time to function, and it does not become clear immediately whether it is beneficial or whether some other approach should be applied.

Moving on: we as humans have a remarkable ability to adapt to changed circumstances, and that can help us greatly in our role as carers. I turn now to explore that quality and how it can help us to come to terms with the challenges Parkinsons presents us with.

I once read about two soldiers in a foxhole in the First World War. One is frightened but uninjured, the other is enduring the torments of the damned as a result of his massive injuries. The uninjured soldier tries to figure out why it is that his comrade-in-arms is in such awful pain, whilst he, lying there in the mud inches away from him, feels none of it.

'I feel your pain' is just a cliché – no you don't, not fully. Empathising with the problems of others is far from easy, especially when you feel burdened with enough issues of your own, and you can feel both overwhelmed and bewildered by the intensity of the feelings being a carer can confront us with.

That point was well made in 1971 by the then leader of the opposition Harold Wilson at the Brighton Labour Party conference. He was addressing the faithful on the subject of unemployment and made this very pertinent observation: 'for the man who is unemployed ... the unemployment percentage is not a statistic, it's not 3.6 per cent seasonally corrected ... for him [it is] 100 per cent.' In the eyes of others your problem may not seem so bad, but for you it is all-consuming, and rightly so.

In the recent Covid epidemic (which as I write is still alive and kicking with a new variant leaking out of South Africa), the extended period of lockdown in 2020 taught us a lot. One particular aspect which soon became apparent was that people quickly adapted themselves to the 'new normal' situation and adapted.

It wasn't particularly pleasant, with isolation clashing with our human desire for contact with others, but we adjusted to the point at which some folk were reluctant to come out of their shells when the lockdown was over and resume life as 'normal'. It was as if lockdown was a kind of comfort blanket which could not easily be discarded.

Funnily enough, I am typing these words early on a Sunday morning as the front porch echoes to the sickening thud of the newspaper hitting the lino with more supplements than your local branch of Holland and Barrett. I decided to take a break from creativity and read the main news section.

On the front page there was a report on precisely this problem of people reluctant to emerge into the daylight after lockdown, and another neologism had been coined which I had not seen before: HOGO.

This acronym stands for the Hassle Of Going Out, and accurately sums up the reluctance of many to come out again into the light of day. An academic commented that socialising was a muscle which needs exercise in order to flourish again.

All this demonstrates that the enormous flexibility and adaptive skills of your average person depends crucially on them being persuaded to flex those psychological muscles, and this is why so many of us do not fight shy of taking on the role of carer and all that it entails.

One of the other curious side-effects of Covid was that we suddenly acquired a whole new vocabulary and quite a few new buzzwords and phrases. One of those has been around for some time: 'not every disability is visible'.

MND (Motor Neurone Disease) is spectacularly visible in its more advanced stages, no more so than in the case of Professor Stephen Hawking, a brilliant mind trapped in a body increasingly debilitated by the disease.

Dementia, on the other hand, is not so easy to spot, for two reasons. First, the scars don't show, as it were. If you are missing two legs after an accident, everyone can see you are disabled, but if your mind is the victim of this disease, it is much harder to detect.

This point was stressed at the height of the lockdown, where some people were excused mask-wearing because of disabilities not all of which were apparent to the casual observer.

None of this is easy, and it doesn't get easier. It is even more challenging when you encounter the ignorance of folk who have not come into contact with a volunteer full-time carer dealing with a seriously challenging situation like yours.

Be tolerant of them, and above all, if they are prepared to listen, talk to them about the pitfalls, challenges and satisfactions involved. Yes, I did write 'satisfactions', as it can be very rewarding when the person you've been caring for recognises, even obliquely, the hard work and love you constantly dedicate to your role.

Chapter ten – Guilty or not guilty?

When the time comes for entry into a care home to be necessary, you are embarking on the most difficult stage of your role as carer.

Here I present you with a challenging paradox which offers you no consolation at all, but it's valid, I assure you. The worse you feel about what is happening, the better and more caring a person you have been throughout the developing situation over many years. Your pain may be acute, and your guilt may well be irrational, extreme even, as it sticks like superglue and is an extremely hard feeling to shake off.

Having to confess that you are unable to struggle any more is not exactly easy either. More than one professional carer and medic has said to me that now is way past time for me to step back, and that most husbands would have given up long ago.

Thanks for the implied complimentary response, but I have the distinct impression that the vast majority of long-term carers who have stayed the course *aren't* most husbands, wives or partners.

They all possess in abundance a special set of qualities and on top of that they draw on their considerable reserves of love in order to try and cope, however bad the situation becomes. That's not much of a consolation, really, but do try and draw some strength and a modest degree of pride from those observations.

That devastating feeling of guilt is something that can almost overwhelm you. If you have been very much in love, the last thing you want to be party to is a decision which causes you and them to be permanently separated from the pleasurable peaks and troughs of daily living close up and personal with them, even though they may have become far too challenging and demanding to manage.

Of course, you can and should visit on a regular basis, and I am mercifully not yet in a situation where my wife no longer recognises me. When that particularly ghastly day dawns, I can as yet offer you no advice based on experience as to how to cope then.

On the one hand, even after that occurs, you will still be drawn to visit, maybe in the false hope that they will have one of those days when they actually realise who you are, but that late stage, when it comes, is something which I both dread and will refer to in a later version of this book whenever it occurs.

I have decided to visit Rusalka at the moment only on alternate days. You may well at this point ask me why. The initial response I would offer is that everyone is different. But that's a bit lame, so I need to tease this out a little more. Apart from giving others in the family an opportunity to go to the nursing home, there is another consideration which you might find uncomfortable even to think about, but you really must come to terms with it.

The care home resident has needs whilst he or she is

well enough to know you, which include wanting to see and hug you and enjoy your presence, but you too have your needs which, if not considered just a little bit, can cause you increasing mental health problems or at the very least to question your own worth.

I am now going to get rather personal. In my own case, I can also find it so distressing to see and talk to her for a couple of hours that I need a day to recuperate. If you think that is implausible, try it on for size when this happens to you. In addition, I have reason to believe that the resident also needs time out from visitors, so that they can adjust more readily to their new environment.

This is where it gets a bit awkward, but bear with me. I also have to carve out a proper life for myself and to have the time and space to engage in activities of my choosing which enable me to feel that life is worthwhile and that I am not just turning into a dutiful and unhappy visitor, but someone who will hopefully enjoy the occasion and make it pleasurable. I hope that makes sense to you.

Re-reading those paragraphs makes it sound more than a touch selfish on my part, but to misquote a royal personage, there are two of us in this marriage and a balance has to be struck. There is no point in visiting every day, facing a crisis yourself as a result and then suddenly taking ill and never turning up again.

The film *The Life of Brian,* which I personally found hilarious, but others may not be so sympathetic about it because of its subject matter ('He's not the Messiah. He's a very naughty boy'), ends with the leading trio each nailed to their cross singing 'Always look on the bright side of life'.

That is one piece of advice I would not agree with in the case of those having to deal with dementia. Some relatives, close or not so close, may insist that their optimistic view of the person you've been caring for is correct, that he or she will certainly settle down permanently at their current level or even improve, and that they would definitely do even better if only their medication or pattern of existence was altered in some ill-defined way.

Optimism is all very well, but when it is misguided, the sense of despair when it is proven wrong can be devastating. I hate to put this down in writing, but one thing about being a pessimist in this kind of situation is that you are never disappointed.

I do not mean to trivialise your feelings, nor to be unsympathetic, but if you know that the person you've cared for is very likely to deteriorate to the point at which they do not recognise who you are, for example, it is foolish to try and give yourself false hope that your experience will be any different from that of countless thousands of others.

I remember talking one day to the manager of the care home where she is now resident, and asking her about Rusalka's condition. She said bluntly, being honest and direct towards me, 'She still has some way to go.'

In other words, given her experience of residents with

dementia and her knowledge of my wife in particular, any plateau she may seem to be currently resting on, so to speak, can and will only be no more than short term.

There is more unpleasantness to come, and there is no way as yet that medical science can either halt or reverse the process. Face up to it and cherish each day when you are recognised and you can still chat about ordinary events and people, and relish your mutual ability to recall past good times.

One significant consolation, surely, is that what you have already enjoyed and experienced together in the past cannot be taken away from you, even though a door has slammed firmly shut on those times and the future is pretty bleak.

I am not religious at all, even though I was a choirboy in the Church of England and have absorbed a great deal of the ceremony and language of the St James's Bible and the Book of Common Prayer. The quote which drifts occasionally into my mind are the Comfortable Words, part of the order for Holy Communion: 'Hear what comfortable words our Saviour Jesus Christ saith to all that truly turn to him: "Come unto me, all ye that travail and are heavy laden, and I will refresh you".' (The text is from St Matthew's gospel.)

I find the use of the English language in these offices quite captivating, but I cannot accept those words of consolation in my own situation, except in the context of the saying 'a problem shared is a problem halved'.

It isn't really, but does help a lot to have a person to whom you can confide your sorrow and confusion, but their sympathy cannot mask or take away the deep-rooted discomfort and pain. In this situation, I find that relatives can be too close to the situation to play this part effectively. They will inevitably base their judgments on their own limited insights into the person you've been so very close to over a long period of time. It can turn into an exchange of clashing views, and that is exactly what isn't needed.

I have a very good friend who has more than once taken time out from an extremely busy public life to sit quietly and allow me to hold forth about my situation and where it is going. He offers me a very welcome handkerchief to cry into, but we both recognise that it is not a panacea.

I have stated more than once in this book that I am not peddling false hope, and I certainly do not presume to offer you a magic bottle of snake oil to cure your ills and those of the person you've cared for.

I am convinced by all I have been through as a carer and now an absentee carer that facing the facts is the best and only way of really coming to terms with the situation. Don't be either an optimist or a pessimist: be a realist instead.

When a loved one actually dies, no words of comfort can take away that painful and irreversible end of a life, but it does mark a clear and decisive cut-off point. If I may say so, I do believe that what happens when they enter a care home is almost a death without a death, if you follow what I am trying to say. It even has been recognised in a piece of medical jargon, namely, 'anticipatory grief', which sums up the dilemma neatly.

Something has been irrevocably taken away from me and no amount of false optimism will bring that back. However, the resident as she used to be lives on in your head and heart, a constant reminder of past years together. In the bitter-sweet words of a classic popular melody by Irving Berlin, 'The Song is ended, but the Memory lingers on'.

One of my research interests has been the impact of two World Wars on twentieth-century Europe. It began when I found a battered copy of *All Quiet on the Western Front* in my grandmother's gaslit house after the floods of 1947, and continued with reading accounts of the war widows created by the next war to end all wars, World War Two, so many of whom had one or more children to bring up alone in the drab austerity of peacetime.

They did not have an army of cognitive therapists queueing up to support them or a string of agony aunts in the Sunday newspapers serving up conflicting advice, they simply got on with the grinding business of living. Their stoicism and grim determination not to be utterly disheartened by their lot is a powerful wake-up call to all of us in these over-pampered times.

That wartime poster, which has become something of a cause celèbre in recent times with its simple legend 'Keep

Calm and Carry On', reflects both their courage in the face of irreversible adversity and our own conflicting emotions as carers of a loved one who is slipping slowly but surely down the slippery slope towards dementia. It is a lesson for all of us today.

Conclusion

And that, as they say, is that. The sound of the fat lady singing can be heard loud and clear. I have told you all that I can in the hope that I may have given help and support to some full-time carers who like me are struggling with their role and emotions and have no idea where to turn.

I do not intend to offer you a long and inscrutable bibliography, as few people ever read them anyway, and my current advice would simply be open up your computer (and if you haven't got one, go to your public library before the local authority closes them all and do it there) and google whatever you need an answer for. Other search engines are also available, but few can compete.

I know: dismissive professionals will tell you not to trust Google or their other bête noire, Wikipedia, as they are 'unreliable' and written by people with an axe to grind. You mean like journalists and politicians, perhaps? Or me, even?

I take the view that most people, especially those who have been full-time carers, have enough savoir faire and common sense to recognise that some web pages are more reliable than others, and that there are seriously conflicting views on just about every subject under the sun, as there always have been. If you can't trust your own judgment, no one else can do it for you. (Politicians please note.)

It brings to mind the misleading mantra chanted at those interminable Covid-19 news conferences and Powerpoint presentations on the telly during the 2020 lockdown, namely, that we must 'follow the science'. That assumes that there is such a thing as a single universal truth which all scientists follow. It is not the case, I'm afraid.

The history of science, from before Galileo and his little run-in with the Inquisition and after, is littered with abundant examples of the vast majority of scientists taking one view, either one vision of a small aspect or of the entirety of life and the universe, which is eventually toppled in favour of the next eternal verity, and so it goes on.

The worst aspect of all this is that it is such an easy trap to fall into to assume that the currently-held orthodoxy must be the right and proper one, because we are all grown up now, we have all the data, we are rational beings more advanced than our predecessors, and so we must be right. Not true. There are generations to come just waiting in the wings, and they will probably be far more capable than us.

Trust your own common sense, do not fall for the dangers of groupthink and mindlessly 'follow the science', but do not be afraid to seek the support and kindness of others. Above all, realise that even though you may be physically isolated, you are not alone.

Many others before you and yet to come will undertake this same tragic journey, caring for your loved one as the slippery slope from Parkinsons into dementia takes place. I wish you well.

A parting shot or two
(More helpful and not-so-helpful quotes)

Do not take life too seriously. You will never get out of it alive.
(Elbert Hubbard)

Always remember that you are unique – just like everybody else.
(Unknown)

Volunteers don't get paid, not because they're worthless, but because they're priceless.
(Sherry Anderson)

Birthdays are good for you. Statistics show that the people who have the most live the longest.
(Larry Lorenzoni)

If I'd known I was going to live this long, I'd have taken better care of myself.
(Anonymous)

Wisdom doesn't necessarily come with age. Sometimes age just shows up all by itself. (Tom Wilson)

Don't ever question the value of volunteers. Noah's Ark was built by volunteers; the Titanic was built by professionals.
(Dave Gynn)

I wondered why somebody didn't do something. Then I realised, I am somebody.
(Unknown)

If you can keep your head when all about you are losing theirs, you don't realise the gravity of the situation.
(A twist on the Rudyard Kipling poem 'If')

We are all here on earth to help others; what on earth the others are here for I don't know.
(W. H. Auden)

Here is a test to find whether your mission on earth is finished: If you're alive it isn't.
(Richard Bach)

I'm too busy working on my own grass to notice if yours is greener.
(Unknown)

People who wonder if the glass is half full or half empty miss the point. The glass is refillable.
(Unknown)

Cinderella is proof that a new pair of shoes can change your life.
(Unknown)

When you come to a fork in the road, take it.
(Yogi Berra)

(Notes: Yogi Berra is a real name, a baseball player famous for his foot in mouth observations. My favourite is his assertion that you should go to other people's funerals, otherwise they won't come to yours. The shoes quotation refers to my wife's collection of footwear which would have made Imelda Marcos jealous.)

Printed in Great Britain
by Amazon